The Breath of God

Nature Formed

Breath Released

Greg Crawford

The Breath of God

All Rights Reserved

Copyrighted 2014 by Greg Crawford

Cover Design by Josh Crawford

No part of this book may be reproduced or transmitted in any form or by any means, graphic, electronic or mechanical, including photocopying, recording, taping, or by any information storage retrieval system, without written permission from the author. The use of short quotes or occasional copying for group study is permitted. All scripture is King James Version

Published by:

Creative Release Publishing

Des Moines, Iowa

thebaseiowa.org

Printed in the United States

First printing 2014

ISBN-13: 978-1494921125

Table of Contents

Introduction vii

Enoch, Friend of God 11

Perfecting That Which is Lacking 33

The Nature of God is Arising 47

The Structure God is Building 51

Four Breaths Seven Glories 67

Four Breaths Seven Glories Overview 115

The Glory and Breath in Acts 121

The Breath of God 135

The Breath As It Comes 159

Greater Works 181

Seven Fold Spirit or Graces 201

Holiness 251

The Journey Begins 277

The Challenge 295

His Nature Formed - His Breath Released

Introduction

I wrote this book because of the need in the Body of Christ to know what God is endeavoring to do in this moment to bring His intentions into the earth. As with all revelations, once revealed, many people are in different seasons. For some, they will progress and perhaps find the ultimate end. Others may struggle. Hopefully this writing will help in bringing clarity and understanding of the dynamics of God's creative power that is beginning to flow and just how large this creative ability is to save nations.

The breath of God is indeed moving in a remnant group. This is a group of pioneers and forerunners of the deep things of the Spirit. This is not to say they are an elitist group but to state that God always deals deep in the heart of someone to carry His emotions into the earth. It is those who have decided to willingly enter into His sufferings so Christ can be formed in them and they can be a tool in His hands.

As God begins to breathe afresh upon His people, we also need to understand He is releasing dynamics of His glory. It is not just a single dynamic but is multi- faceted. His breath lifts us, moves us, carries us and transforms us to be both participators in this glory and for this glory to be released into the earth.

This writing is for those who desire to press into the deep things of God, the extreme things of God and have understanding of those things in a way to convey these ways of God to others. If ever we are to be encouraged in the season we are living in, it is now. Knowing the ways of God helps us to see clearly and enables us to partner precisely with Him.

The Breath of God

His Nature Formed - His Breath Released

Chapter 1

Enoch, Friend of God

How did the men of old... the revivalists, become so close to God? So many names! Here are a few to trigger your thoughts. Perhaps you have not heard of all of them.

Smith Wigglesworth, Charles Finney, Jack Coe, John Alexander Dowie, Maria Woodworth-Etter, John G. Lake, Andrew Murray, David Brainerd, Aimee Semple McPherson, George Fox, Elizabeth Fry, John Hus, Lester Sumrall, Billy Sunday, George Whitefield, Leonard Ravenhill, William Booth, William Seymour, Charles Parham, George Warnock (Latter Rain), Martha Robinson (1874 Radiant Glory), Charles Brown & John Bates (Iowa Band), A.A. Allen, William Branham, Evan Roberts, Kathryn Kuhlman, etc.

What is the missing element of today? Why are we not seeing this type of sold out leaders coming forth, or are we? God is doing some amazing things deep in the hidden recesses of a remnant people in this hour. They desire one thing and it is that Christ be glorified in and through them. They are not looking for fame or large crowds. They are not concerned about the flattery of men or even man's affirmation. They are in a process. A process that is dear to God because once completed, it will help bring the end of this present age and birth the eternal age.

Philippians 1:20–26 (KJV 1900) — *20 According to my earnest expectation and my hope, that in nothing I shall be ashamed, but that with all boldness, as always, so now also Christ shall be magnified in my body, whether it be by life, or by death. 21 For to me to live is Christ, and to die is gain. 22 But if I live in the flesh, this is the fruit of my labour: yet what I shall choose I wot not. 23 For I am in a strait betwixt two, having a desire to depart, and to be with Christ; which is far better: 24 Nevertheless to abide in the flesh is more needful for you. 25 And having this confidence, I know that I shall abide and continue with you all for your furtherance and joy of faith; 26 That your rejoicing may be more abundant in Jesus Christ for me by my coming to you again.*

What caused this transformation inside that allowed God's glory to come? It wasn't an anointing. It wasn't a certain prayer. It wasn't worship. It was a deep wrestling and anguish of soul. It was a final decision to fully yield and then allow God to begin a process. This was a process that was beyond knowledge but would allow the very nature of God to become resident within their life and soul. We talk of God coming and abiding but we only talk of it occurring in large gatherings. It's as if the large size of the group will help hide us

The Breath of God

and our shortcomings so we can enjoy His presence without paying any price. The pursuit of the nature of God will extract a price from you that will far exceed any sacrifice you have done in times past.

You see it is not a matter of knowledge about God or even the truths of God; we are talking about His nature. Yes, it is the fruit of the Spirit. Yes, it is the gifts of the Spirit. But in reality, it is the seven fold nature of *Isaiah 11:1-3.* The seven graces of God working in our lives creating change deep within.

I had a vision of the flame of God. There was a courtyard and I entered it through a large gate. In the middle was a large round wall that would remind you of a large well. But inside this wall and burning about 50 feet into the air was a supernatural flame. It was multi-colored. It bounced and leaped and seemed alive. I knew it was a pathway into heaven, a portal that gave access. As I walked closer to it, I also realized the flame went the opposite way, seemingly into the earth. It was a portal into the bowels of hell as well. The same flame was at the entrance point of both heaven and hell.

This seemed strange to me that the two could be connected by the same flame or fire. It also seemed in the vision that everyone had to come through the gate and into this courtyard and would experience this moment. As I stood in these visions watching the flame and desiring to step in to gain access to heaven, the Lord spoke to me and asked me a simple question. "Can your life pass through the flame?" it caught me off guard and in a moment of time I knew the meaning. There were angels stationed around the courtyard as guardians of the flame. They turned to me and said "Everyone accessing heaven: their life must pass through the flame and if it does, it lifts them to heaven. But if their life does not pass through the flame, the same flame takes them to hell." It was a very sobering thought. I reasoned this was not about anointing or gifting or knowledge of God. It came to me in a moment of time. All of these things were borrowed from God to do the work. No, the only thing that would pass through the flame would be His nature!.

This vision has led me on a path of making sure my life would pass through the flame. I also see so many others striving for all the things in God but not really striving for Him. I wonder how many lives today think they will pass through the flame when in reality, Jesus will say 'away from me' because He did not really know us.

Matthew 3:16–17 (KJV 1900) — 16 And Jesus, when he was baptized, went up straightway out of the water: and, lo, the heavens were opened unto him, and he saw the Spirit of God descending like a dove, and lighting upon him:

The Breath of God

17 And lo a voice from heaven, saying, This is my beloved Son, in whom I am well pleased.

What pleases the heart of God is when His nature is magnified. Jesus came to be water baptized. John voiced that He is the chosen One. So many times we only look at this and say the Father was pleased with Jesus. But in all reality, He was pleased with John as well. He was also saying 'this is my beloved son, John, hear him. John then states that He (Jesus) must increase and John must decrease. The Father was completely satisfied. The nature of Himself was walking upon the earth and about to become the witness or living testimony of what that nature could do through a yielded human vessel.

The Glory descends whenever we make a heart felt decision of spiritual advancement.

- The Glory came when Moses went up the Mount.
- The Glory came when Jesus went to the Cross.
- The Glory came when Paul was confronted on the road.
- The Glory came when Solomon built the temple.
- The Glory came when they gathered in the upper room
- The Glory came ... in your life every time you made a decision to move forward.

Our decisions are not about the things we have decided to embrace or change or do. No, they really come down to one thing; they always confront us to see more of God's nature in our lives. It is when we allow Christ to be formed in us .... to strike the vision that brings God's pleasure and God's satisfaction through our life.

2 Corinthians 5:1–4 (KJV 1900) — 1 For we know that if our earthly house of this tabernacle were dissolved, we have a building of God, an house not made with hands, eternal in the heavens. 2 For in this we groan, earnestly desiring to be clothed upon with our house which is from heaven: 3 If so be that being clothed we shall not be found naked. 4 For we that are in this tabernacle do groan, being burdened: not for that we would be unclothed, but clothed upon, that mortality might be swallowed up of life.

Are you burdened? Not with cares of the world or how to pay your bills, or to have more time or whatever you're fighting by faith. Are you burdened with the lost? Are you burdened with the injustice in the world? Are you burdened to see a sweeping move of God? All of these are most admirable and things we should all be believing for. But one thing will touch all these things. Are you burdened to be clothed from on High? To be mantled --- not with gifting--- not with a ministry

The Breath of God

or calling ---- but to be clothed with His nature!

Clothed means 'to sink into a garment, to be endued, to lie in wait'. Are we so busy running for God we are not waiting for him to truly clothe us from on high? To mantle us not with gifting or abilities but with His nature. I see so many people so caught up in busyness and having little to no real nature of God. You see, once we have the nature, we have all things pertaining to holiness and godliness. We have what it takes to not work at change but to actually bring the agent of change. You see, the nature in itself will cause men to weep and hearts to turn without a word preached. It will cause repentance of soul to be felt without the begging and convincing of the need of Christ.

Charles Finney would get on a train and before long, the whole train would fall under conviction and begin to weep not knowing what was going on. It was not the anointing or preaching doing this but the nature of God that he carried. I know a man today who is carrying this same nature of God. He pulled up to a gas pump to fill his truck and the man on the other pump began to weep uncontrollably. He finally came over to him, drawn by the nature of God. He said "I don't know what is going on or who you are, but there is something about you that is causing me to see myself for the vile person I really am. I cannot seem to hide it and my heart feels as if it is naked." This is what the nature of God will do!

So what is the disconnect? What is keeping us from the life we know we can live and the life we currently are living? It is because we have not yet been clothed from on High.

Hebrews 11:5 (KJV 1900) — 5 By faith Enoch was translated that he should not see death; and was not found, because God had translated him: for before his translation he had this testimony, that he pleased God.

The Lord had me meditating on Enoch and how he walked with Him, pleased him and was no more. I came to some conclusions after reading about him. Enoch is mentioned in **Genesis 4** and **5**. There are only three N.T. verses about him so where was I reading? The book of Enoch. Yes, an entire book about him, it's just not canonized. The thing about Enoch that is amazing is how much God showed him about exactly how creation works and God's interaction with it. He was to bring this to earth for men to know but men rejected him. After repeatedly trying to share this over a period of time, God decided to "take him" as he was in heaven again, God decided no sense in returning, just stay here!

Now I bring Enoch up because there were only two men in scripture that says 'they pleased God' and one who God said he was pleased with. Of course that one is Jesus when he said "this is my beloved Son in whom I am well pleased". The other two were Noah and Enoch. So let's look at Enoch as we can easily see Noah's life.

Probably the main point that we see with Enoch's life and that we talk about constantly is the fact that he did not die but that God took him. We assume that he was plucked off the earth because of how pleasing his life was to God. This is probably furthest from the truth of what really happened. Enoch was about living in the eternity of God and not a temporal view of the world. He had positioned himself into the eternal realm. This enabled him to be in a position to never experience death.

The Latter Rain movement of the 1940's and 50's also believed that you could come to that place and not experienced death. Out of the 13 points the Latter Rain movement believed, we practice 12 of those points today. The 13th point of living eternally and not experiencing death was rejected by the majority of the Church thus the Latter Rain movement was looked at as a movement of heresy. Perhaps they had some piece of understanding about the eternal realm that we are lacking today.

Enoch was also about seeing the mysteries in revelation of God's heart to redeem the earth and reform it or shift it back to God's original intention for humanity. This is why he was able to see how heaven was interacting with the earth and how all creation was groaning for the manifestation of the sons and daughters of God. Enoch became a living example of how the eternal soul of man would be translated to heaven.

His life was a life that superseded time and space. He was living a life not just <u>in</u> the miracles of God but <u>being</u> the miracle of God. He had been anointed to go into the revelatory realm and God could entrust him these great mysteries of creation. Enoch's unique call and experience is nothing more than a reflection of his willingness to yield to the spirit of God and to reflect the nature of God as well.

For us to be redeemed today and to experience salvation, the highest price was paid dealing with the human nature that we allow to hold us back. Enoch somehow glimpsed salvation and redemption and was able to take authority over his human nature and allow the nature of God to be so formed in him that God was sharing part of His nature. It was the nature of God inside Enoch!

As we look for just a moment at Noah's life, we also see a pattern that has emerged. Noah was a direct descendent of Enoch. Noah is believed to have written the book of Enoch and recorded his thoughts. So Enoch sees creation and Noah was trusted to save God's creation. No wonder that we read in **Romans 8** that the earth is groaning waiting for the manifestation of the sons of God.

Enoch had a son, Methuselah. When he was born, his face was aglow and his eyes were a flame of fire. The very nature of God was evident within him. So much like a created being, it is said he had the appearance like an angel. So Enoch named him Methuselah, which means *'who is of God'*. The nature of God so prevalent in Enoch that his offspring took on that nature at birth. Now that is powerful!

Enoch means '*dedicated one*'. So God in this hour is looking for a remnant to come forth unlike any other seen. He is looking for some "dedicated ones" to birth some "who is like God" glowing with the nature of God. They are burning with His holiness and fire. Whose lives from birth will pass through the flame. It is a birthing or bringing forth of that which is truly eternal.

They will be ones who just don't complete assignments, but we will be burdened with the same things that are burdening the heart of God. It is an anointing to spare the earth and the people of the earth. They, as Melchisedec priests, like Enoch, will be able to access heaven to implement and shift the earth. They will truly know how to walk "with" God as His nature is within them.

Genesis 5:18-24 [18] Jared lived one hundred and sixty-two years, and begot Enoch. [19] After he begot Enoch, Jared lived eight hundred years, and had sons and daughters. [20] So all the days of Jared were nine hundred and sixty-two

years; and he died. [21] Enoch lived sixty-five years, and begot Methuselah. [22] After he begot Methuselah, <u>Enoch walked with God three hundred years, and had sons and daughters.</u> [23] So all the days of Enoch were three hundred and sixty-five years. [24] <u>And Enoch walked with God</u>; and he was not, for God took him.

We don't understand the condition of the earth at the time of Enoch. Men were evil and doing all kinds of evil things ..... yet Enoch walked with God. Men stopped following God and even denounced him .... Yet Enoch walked with God. Men refused to listen to God or His messengers ---- Yet Enoch walked with God. Sounds a lot like the day we live in now, doesn't it? Yet Enoch not only sustained his faith in God, he walked with God. Much like Adam walked with God in the cool of the garden. You see the nature of God in Enoch enabled him to experience a type of redemption that brought the original intention of God back to the earth.

The word 'walk' means several different things. It means *'go, to proceed, to die, the manner of life'*, and is associated with the word *yalak which* means *'to follow, be carried or brought, to depart,* **<u>to ascend and return - to appear to die and return</u>**'. I like the underlined and bold definition best. To walk with God is to have His nature resurrected inside of you! It seems that from this definition, Enoch and the others who walked so close to God actually died to self so completely that the nature of God was all that was seen in them. In Enoch's case, he actually fulfilled this definition to "*ascend and return*". This seems to be the desire of God that Christ ascended and now returns with His nature to live in each of as believers.

Let's look at the word '*with*'. It means '*together with, in relationship with, to meet, encounter, approach, be opportune, to allow to meet, cause to meet, to be sent, be allowed to meet, to seek occasion, cause oneself to meet*'.

His way of walking "*causes him to meet*" God! Something has brought a union or a reason for communion. Or, the relationship came to the point he met God and as he met God, he was able to maintain the relationship. It was a perpetual binary moment of one creating and sustaining the other.

To walk BEFORE God was a life of devotion. The appearance before the throne. Many Christians are very devoted. Be it from obligation, wrong fear of God or desire coming from appreciation by being free from sin. But to walk with God is completely different. To WALK WITH God was a life of constant communion. It was being in the *Shekinah* Glory of God. Now Enoch walked almost his whole life this way. He walked in the *Shekinah* 300 years!

His Nature Formed - His Breath Released

Revelations that come from God have a degree of glory surrounding them. That glory is hiding them. But as we learn to walk with God, we have access to them. We are able to go beyond the veiling of the glory and to see them in the midst of the glory.

I had a vision that occurred several times. I saw a great mountain that we were to ascend. There were two ways of ascending: straight up the side or to take the trail that went around and around. Many were taking the trail, but I and a few others decided to ascend straight up the side. We saw this great fire burning at the top. It was a fire that was enfolding upon itself and was the most brilliant orange glow. It was illuminating the mountain even in the darkness. But it seemingly was hidden to those taking the winding path as they were tucked into the mountain where the mountain itself hid the glowing image. For those of us ascending straight up, we were out on a rocky ridge and held the view of the fire in our sight. As we ascended, I knew what we desired to see was the glory of God. It was there before our eyes and kept us driving ever higher. When we were about to reach the summit, I knew we would be able to touch it and the awe of what we were about to see seemed overwhelming. As we crested the top and began to stand up on the highest peak, I looked down the mountain and knew we had a hard climb. I saw the multitude still trying to traverse the beaten path unwilling to get off what had become common. Many were tired and worn out and many had even died along the way, yet they had only gotten half way up. What was worse is they had not yet seen what we had peered upon for such a long time. How sad to spend your life and still not see what you know in your spirit exists. I looked back at what my eyes had desired- His glory! The Lord then spoke and said, "This is not yet My glory but only the reflection coming from it!" I could then see the true glory resting in the distance and knew we were only standing in its shadow, yet the shadow of it was brighter than the sun. The Lord then spoke again and said, "Many stop at this point and believe what they have found is all of me but the vastness of my glory is endless and all eternity will be required to find it."

The walk of Enoch was a walk of intimate communion. It was a walk of ascending and descending. It was a walk that brought him not just to the crest of the mountain but to the real glory. You see, once he got up the mountain the first time, he then had the communion or relationship with the Lord so that each time he ascended; the Lord was there with him. The journey became easier as he was making his own path upward and began to know exactly when and what steps were needed.

When two friends thus walk together, their communion is secret. So is the communion between you and God. When I speak, I tell a lot of what God does in secret with me so others will understand God. Some things I don't share and some things I have never shared. Without the experiences in God matching up to our doctrines in God, all we have is head knowledge that is far from a life of reality. God wants to not just walk through life with us like a distant acquaintance but to walk so close He can tell us the secrets behind life itself.

When two friends thus walk together, their conversation is on the same level as well. God looks at us as friends and does not talk down to us. He longs to share His secrets with a people that have His nature residing within. Because to have His nature means you always cherish Him above all things and cherish His nature as well. When we are in that position, then God will entrust to us the true riches, the hidden riches and things revealing how His ways operate.

When two friends thus walk together, their wills and governing feelings are the same; for how "can two walk together except they be agreed?" In other words, they have the same desires, passions, vision, and assignments. The driving force behind each of their actions is the same. They also keep the same course and so are advancing towards the same objective. Imagine if the Body of Christ was doing this! Imagine what could be accomplished in such a short time.

The Breath of God

When Enoch had come to a certain point, the Word says God took him and he was no more. We can interpret this in two ways. With the understanding we have gained of the word 'walk' meaning '*to ascend and return -- to appear to die and return*'. We could interpret this to mean that Enoch no longer appeared but the nature of God appeared in him!

We typically look at the story in the way of God literally taking him. The word 'took' means '*to lay hold of or seize, to take away*'. This can mean his physical body or it could mean his sinful nature. I believe it has a double meaning. Of both HE was no more and God seized him and he no longer was on the earth. I believe the first had to occur for the second to happen. After all, only the redeemed with the nature of God will make heaven.

The friendship God had with Enoch was so close he literally seized him. God decided the value of Enoch was so great He could not bear to have him leave. Enoch had seen so much of God that he knew much about God's ways and desires. He had seen so much of what God intended and how God moved. He had seen angels and Seraphim and Cherubim and he also saw Ophannim. Ophannim means 'the wheels of Ezekiel' personified!

But of all the things Enoch saw, he also saw one more thing. He saw his identity in Heaven, He saw His value. In the book of Enoch, here's what he actually said, "the Lord opened his eyes to see who he was in heaven". Now imagine that, not who he was in the earth but who he was in Heaven! His value in heaven! Has God opened your eyes to see your value in heaven? God has been speaking to me about these very things. Something so eternal that the temporal truly seems of no importance at all. God desires to open your eyes so you can see who you are! It is the Spirit of Understanding that was loosed at Pentecost. It is the Spirit that searches the deep things of God.

The Lord in a visitation spoke to me and said "I am bringing you into a place like Enoch; I am going to show you things by revelation. I have showed you the revelation that I knew others would reject. I have given you a part of My heart knowing you would honour Me and cherish what I have given. You seek for everyone to come and hear what I have given you but I already know that many will not come. Is it not enough I have given this revelation to you? Is it not enough to know the privilege I have given you in knowing My revelation? I am your reward and nothing else matters."

Hebrews 11:5 *By faith Enoch was taken away so that he did not see death, "and was not found, because God had taken him"; for before he was taken he had this testimony, that he pleased God.*

In three words, Enoch's entire life is summed up: He pleased God! The word 'pleased' is only used three times in scripture. It's used twice in talking about Enoch in reference to Enoch and one other time about people who are walking according to righteousness. It's not used any other time in scripture. Here he is listed in the hallmark of faith chapter. As we look at his life, we can conclude three things about his faith:

A. Enoch's faith pleased God.
B. Enoch's faith produced a proper testimony.
C. Enoch's faith protected his fellowship with God in a sinful   society.

So Enoch was translated. The word 'translated' is a tremendous word.

Translated = *metatithemi* /met·at·**ith**·ay·mee/ to carry over, to transfer, **To abandon loyalty to, almost always associated with laying on of Hands**

   Meta means - amongst

   Titehemi means - to appoint or make

It was a mutual translation. God did not just decide to take him but actually because of the relationship they had, it was a mutual decision. This is why Paul said he could go on to be with the Lord or stay and that staying was more profitable for us. He was at the same point in his walk with the Lord that all he had to do was decide and I believe he, too would have been no more!

You see, Enoch walked so close to God. Being translated was because God's hand was literally upon him and when God's hand withdrew, he was so connected he withdrew <u>IN THE HAND OF GOD!</u>

What caused this? The Bible clearly says his life PLEASED God. Now let's look at what his life produced that enabled this. The word 'please' means '*to be well pleasing, to be well pleased with a thing*'.

It comes from a root word meaning '*acceptable*'. It does not mean how we act or what we do. The actually meaning is almost entirely not about us but how others view us. The one person here we are concerned about is how does God view us. So when we put the word 'please' into the context of who is to be pleased, it means **how God views men's** actions and behavior. It is **God's attitude towards human behavior.** It is the standard of righteousness God uses to measure us. Not measuring ourselves or comparing ourselves but allowing God to measure us and to determine if what we do pleases Him or not.

Every time I minister, or sit in a service while others minister, or lead a series of services, I ask God this simple question "Were You pleased?" It does not matter if the people are pleased or if I am pleased. It only matters if God is pleased. I will tell you it is not fun to be on the wrong side of that answer! As a leader, I take very seriously the role of leading and being responsible for what was allowed or not accomplished. It grieves my spirit. I

The Breath of God

have had to wrestle through many times when God was not pleased. I have repented for not leading or failing to lead. I seek the Holy Spirit until I get the answers of when the turn was wrong or what occurred that was not the intention of God. I need to know for the next time to be more in tune with Him. Without asking this simple question, we jump to assumptions that God is pleased when in reality, He may not be at all. It's like I have told my people, sometimes we need to leave services not feeling good at all because God is dealing deep in us. That is when the greatest joy is probably brought to the heart of God.

Jude 1:14-15 [14] Now Enoch, the seventh from Adam, prophesied about these men also, saying, "Behold, the Lord comes with ten thousands of His saints, [15] to execute judgment on all, to convict all who are ungodly among them of all their ungodly deeds which they have committed in an ungodly way, and of all the harsh things which ungodly sinners have spoken against Him."

What God's nature in us does is makes us to be true proclaimers of truth in the midst of a perverse and wicked world. It is like fire shut up in our bones, it is the nature of God, not an anointing. It is residue upon the locks of the door that draws us ever closer.

You see Enoch proclaimed the Second Coming, Enoch proclaimed judgment to the ungodly and he

His Nature Formed - His Breath Released

talked of how their works, deeds and words would be exposed. We find Enoch preaching a hard message for a hardened people. It will take Enochs with the nature of God in this hour, to turn the hardness of the hearts in our Nation.

Chapter 2

Perfecting That Which is Lacking

1 Thessalonians 3:10-11 (KJV 1900) — 10 Night and day praying exceedingly that we might see your face, and might perfect that which is lacking in your faith? 11 Now God himself and our Father, and our Lord Jesus Christ, direct our way unto you.

Paul saw something that was lacking in the faith of the Thessalonians. As a spiritual father, he did not want them to become stagnant or fail in their journey with God. He had invested into their lives and knew the forward motion had stopped. He was praying night and day for a way to see them. He knew he could not change the situation that existed by simply praying but it would only shift by going!

Paul also understood he had the answer for them and it was resident inside of him. He could not send Timothy or another spiritual son but he himself would need to go. He also alludes to "we" meaning Paul had engaged others for this prayer focus and had determined they, too would be going. Paul probably used it as a teaching assignment for both those present with him and for those he was addressing.

Paul said in his writings "follow me as I follow Christ". These seem like simple words but they are more than a doctrinal stance or belief system, or even the manner of life Paul alluded to many times. It was the process of Christ being formed in him so that He would be found in him. Paul was not going to the Thessalonians to simply convey more truth. He was going to confront what was lacking. He was going to perfect it! The truth they held fast to was stagnant. The process of Christ being formed had come to a halt. The only thing Paul had that could perfect them was not just truth since it is optional to receive or open to private interpretation. No, Paul was going to bring the very nature of God to confront them. The nature of God that is perfect. The nature of God that is the basis for all truth. Paul knew only God's nature could perfect that which was lacking.

They had come to a place of needing a missing ingredient. We have come to the place of a missing ingredient as well in the Church. There was a certain stillness they were experiencing that needed to be confronted, much like the stillness we are experiencing.

This would not shift by revival meetings or outpouring meetings, etc. The only way to gain the cultural voice as the "Church" is not to entertain the world but for the world to be confronted by the very nature of God.

"And he said, Go forth, and stand upon the mount before the Lord. And, behold, the Lord passed by, and a great and strong wind rent the mountains, and brake in pieces the rocks before the Lord; but the Lord was not in the wind: and after the wind an earthquake; but the Lord was not in the earthquake; and after the earthquake a fire; but the Lord was not in the fire: and after the fire a still small voice" (1 Kings 19:11-12).

Elijah had come to the same place of the seeming stillness of God, part of it was his own doing by the decision he made and part of it was God allowing him to come to the end of himself. He had just experienced great success as he had defeated the false prophets by calling fire down. He had survived the drought in the land. He had seen the rain of God come and he supernaturally outran the chariot. Yet in the midst of this high point, he still had dissatisfaction within himself. He seemed to believe he had less power than the Jezebel he was facing.

He was in a seemingly hidden and nsignificant place. Yet what seems insignificant in our lives is sometimes the deepest places God is building something in us. Something so deep it will be able to confront all our situations including our own lack of confidence. These places are where character is formed and God's dealings bring us to the end of ourselves. These places are opportunities, opportunities for enlargement of the nature of God within us.

Human nature desires to give up. It becomes complacent and despondent. It decides to settle for what has been or what is. It also stops putting a demand on our faith. Paul understood this and saw it happening with the Thessalonians. They were in a battle not with principalities or circumstances, but an internal battle. The same type of battle we all face, a battle of wills. It is actually the ultimate battle; will Christ be fully formed in us?

It is easy for us to embrace concepts about God and even truth about God. It is also easy to put those things into action. We move along in our Christian walk over years allowing the forming process of those truths to become a part of us. We have a pretty good grip on our Christian faith until we hit a hidden wall. The forming process of Christ in us, the hope of glory reaches a pivotal point, a tipping point. Will we allow the process to take on a new depth, another dimension? Will we yield and allow our lives to go through His fire, His purging, His purifying? Can our life pass through the flame and survive?

2 Corinthians 10:3–5 (KJV 1900) — *3 For though we walk in the flesh, we do not war after the flesh: 4 (For the weapons of our warfare are not carnal, but mighty through God to the pulling down of strong holds;) 5 Casting down imaginations, and every high thing that exalteth itself against the knowledge of God, and bringing into captivity every thought to the obedience of Christ;*

As Christians, we tend to put false finish lines into our lives which are only indicators of work or truth attained and not the ultimate conclusion. The ultimate battle is to enter into victorious manners of sustained life. It is not to live in victory or have victory, even thought that is part of it. It is living in rest, living in healing, walking in life abundantly and doing the greater works. It is no longer I that lives but Christ living through me. Few find this pathway in God but in this hour, this is the call of so many. Revelation has come to us and through us at the highest level. Just like the Word made flesh and dwelt among us. It then puts a demand on the nature of man to abandon self and let Christ live through us. This is the intention of God in this hour to truly have the Bride without spot or wrinkle.

Galatians 2:20 (KJV 1900) — *20 I am crucified with Christ: nevertheless I live; yet not I, but Christ liveth in me: and the life which I now live in the flesh I live by the faith of the Son of God, who loved me, and gave himself for me.*

The dilemma is not the circumstances we face, it is whether we will accept the position we have. We want all from God that we can get or so it seems, until He asks for all of us for Christ to be perfectly formed in us. Paul told the Galatians is was not about truths or concepts or doctrine but Christ living inside of him. That is why he said "follow me as I follow Christ". He was saying more than how he lived his life but Who lived through his life. Now that's a new and living way!

Galatians 3:1–4 (KJV 1900) — *1 O foolish Galatians, who hath bewitched you, that ye should not obey the truth, before whose eyes Jesus Christ hath been evidently set forth, crucified among you? 2 This only would I learn of you, Received ye the Spirit by the works of the law, or by the hearing of faith? 3 Are ye so foolish? having begun in the Spirit, are ye now made perfect by the flesh? 4 Have ye suffered so many things in vain? if it be yet in vain.*

So back to the ultimate battle. What are we battling for? What are we laboring for? What are we investing into that is not fully satisfying us? The question is what does Christ want us to battle? What is He endeavoring to fight for? He is battling and desires us to battle for His life to be formed in us. What Christ is building is a people living in a sustained flow of life from Him.

That is where the ultimate battle is being fought..... All other things are simple distractions.

1 Corinthians 2:9–16 (KJV 1900) — 9 But as it is written, Eye hath not seen, nor ear heard, neither have entered into the heart of man, the things which God hath prepared for them that love him. 10 But God hath revealed them unto us by his Spirit: for the Spirit searcheth all things, yea, the deep things of God. 11 For what man knoweth the things of a man, save the spirit of man which is in him? even so the things of God knoweth no man, but the Spirit of God. 12 Now we have received, not the spirit of the world, but the spirit which is of God; that we might know the things that are freely given to us of God. 13 Which things also we speak, not in the words which man's wisdom teacheth, but which the Holy Ghost teacheth; comparing spiritual things with spiritual. 14 But the natural man receiveth not the things of the Spirit of God: for they are foolishness unto him: neither can he know them, because they are spiritually discerned. 15 But he that is spiritual judgeth all things, yet he himself is judged of no man. 16 For who hath known the mind of the Lord, that he may instruct him? But we have the mind of Christ.

Paul begins to show the great mystery of Christ in us the hope of Glory. In verse 13, he says "comparing spiritual things with spiritual". Let's look at these words.

The word 'comparing' means '*joining*'. But the words 'spiritual' are not the same definition. The first word 'spiritual' means '*that which comes from the spirit, that which is manifest*'. The second word 'spiritual' means '*one who possesses the spirit (pneuma, life) of God*'. We cannot join what is from the Spirit to our flesh. It only connects to our redeemed spirit or the nature of God. God does not attach Himself except to Himself or His nature.

Then what is received is not a concept but becomes part of them, it is engrafted in. It comes from the Spirit for the one purpose that it merges with our spirit. That's why in Verse 16, Paul says we have "*the mind of Christ*". The word 'mind' is not so much intellect but means '*manner of life, way of thinking*'. You see God gives us His intentions or His intentions become alive as the nature is made perfect or to the fullness in us. It is not a reprogramming of our existing mind but receiving the sent manner of life Christ gives us. It is His nature releasing His thoughts concerning our actions.

The mind of Christ automatically comes with His nature. The mind of Christ becomes activated by the Spirit living within us (internal) not us experiencing the Spirit's activity towards us (external). His manner of life is what He is building. But do we have His manner of life?

An easy way to determine this is how we pray. I hear most prayer coming from a 'still being redeemed' nature. It has an outside looking in focus, a begging or asking without confidence. Look at the prayers Jesus prayed and then hear how others now pray. Jesus prayed from the nature of God within Him. I describe it like this: His prayers were conversations with His Father that He let us hear. Spirit to Spirit. Nature to Nature and also the exchange back to Him from heaven. Most of what we pray is partial nature to nature and even then, we are only hearing in part because the fullness cannot come unless there is more of Christ formed in us.

Galatians 4:19 (KJV 1900) — *19 My little children, of whom I travail in birth again until Christ be formed in you,*

The word 'form' means = *to strike the vision, a*

part assigned, destiny

Paul travailed a second time, the first for their salvation the beginning of Christ in them and then that He would be formed in them. Paul was battling for one thing.... that the people of God would take on the exact vision of Christ. Not a vision of the future but that they would be the vision of Christ. That if you looked on them, you looked on Christ.

So what does this vision look like? It is the proclamation of the manner of life. It is not just the proclamation of truth. That's what most of Christianity is doing today, giving truth and then trying to convince others of that truth. The proclamation of the manner of life is showing the outcome of how Christ empowers us to live life. It is the demonstration of the manner of life.

That is why Paul said "*I don't come to you with words of man's wisdom but with demonstration of power*". The word 'power' means "*dunamis*" which in the bottom line definition means '*the nature of God*'. Paul did not confront with truth or memorized answers like we do today but he confronted with the very nature of God bringing truth. The words came from deep within his spirit. They flowed like a river of living water from the nature of Christ within! Imagine today if we had the nature formed in us and we ministered from that nature.

Many will say 'I am doing that'! No, for the most part, we are ministering in anointing but not His nature. We are giving memorized verses and not the Word alive and sharper than any two edged sword.

Now back to the Thessalonians, Paul prayed for a way to be opened so he could see them face to face. He knew that the only way to truly move them from the place they were to the place that Christ would be formed or the vision would be struck was they needed to see the vision again. They needed to see the nature of God present. Paul knew the nature was inside. Greater is He than he that is in the world. He knew his presence would actually be HIS presence standing before them. He knew HIS nature would confront all doubts and ignite their hearts again!

Now imagine today how the Church is just like this in so many ways. Stuck in truth and all the dynamics of truth but not much nature. The Truth but not much manifestation of it. What is coming is God is forming His nature in a more perfect way in many people. Many are having to go through the deep dealings of God. Not the wrestling of truth to decide to embrace it or not, but whether they will yield completely and their life will no longer be their own. For those who do, they will be the manifest sons and daughters the whole earth is groaning for. You see, even creation knows the nature. It was formed from it. It also has seen the nature hanging on a cross and redeemed mankind. The whole earth knows that when these sons and daughters begin to manifest that nature, the redeemed plan of God for the whole earth will begin to unfold. The nature of God has the ability to create. It has the ability to redeem. It has the ability to restore.

His Nature Formed - His Breath Released

Chapter 3

The Nature of God is Arising

This is a prophetic word I received in September 2012.

Arise, Arise, Arise My Church! Arise in My nature! For there is coming shortly an arising not of men and women, and not even of men and women who have died to selfish ambition, but there is coming an arising of My very nature upon the earth. For when My nature arises, who can stand before its mighty depths? It has shifted nations and confronted the hearts of kings. My nature will contend without contending. It will cause hearts to repent without preaching. It will cause demons to flee without decree. The hiding of sin in hearts will be exposed and the freedom of My nature will cause a willingness in hearts to announce their need of Me. Arise in My nature! Arise by my nature. Arise fulfilling My nature. But you say 'what of those who are dying to self in this hour? Are they not in a process of death that I can be seen through them? Yes, I am perfecting death, to perfect My nature. Just as My Son's nature was perfected in death to manifest in life in resurrection. Don't you know all who die in this hour will be resurrected in My nature? A power will be released through the cost of their lives that will set in motion the full manifestation of My nature upon the earth. This is what happened after My Son's death, a full manifestation then could be seen. There is coming an arising of My nature that has not been seen in this generation who cries out and longs for more than the simplicity of anointing. They are crying in their souls to be transformed and changed and to walk in what is divine and full. Don't you hear the cry of hearts in this hour? Hearing this cry is the way into the death process. It is the doorway, it is the invitation. Without it, the depths of death will not be realized or found. Who will go for Me? Who will be My voice? Who will release My presence? Who will be My nature upon the earth? This is what is arising in this hour: the seeds of My nature that have been nurtured in the secret place. For some, they have held fast to these seeds for years. For others, only a short while. But none is less or more. Don't you know that when My nature arises, that so many questions will be answered? So many concerned hearts will be met. So many things will fail in contrast to My glory. For My nature will be encompassed by My glory. This is how you will tell what is

The Breath of God

truly Divine. So take heart this day that My nature is what is beginning to arise. It is truly what all seek.

His Nature Formed - His Breath Released

Chapter 4

The Structure God is Building

Exodus 25:8 *"And let them make me a sanctuary; that I may dwell among them."*

Exodus 25:40 *"And look that thou make them after their pattern, which was shewed thee in the mount."*

Moses received a pattern on the mountain. It was to build a dwelling place for God upon the earth. As I look around, I see a lot of building of all kinds of things but I honestly don't see the true thing God intends to build. What we seem to be doing is mimicking the past instead of allowing God to create the future through us.

Our frustrations come because we are trying to restore something that resembles the Glory. It has certain dynamics. It contains the truths of God. It also has His presence at times, the anointing and maybe even the gifts of the Spirit. But the question is, does it have the life of God? Is it carrying His breath deep within it? Are we pursuing all the elements and we have forsaken pursuing Him? When we become consumed to find the Glory, we miss the greater intentions of God. All these other things will be added when we seek Him and His kingdom.

Haggai 2:9 *"the glory of this latter house shall be greater than of the former"*

The former covenant was ushered in with glory but was doomed to pass away. It was the plan of God to point to and reveal a greater glory yet to come. A glory that was so full of the life of God that all men would be confronted by it and desire it. The new covenant was not destined to burst forth gloriously and fade away. It was destined to burst forth and have a continuation of glory. This glory can only be found in the face of Jesus Christ. The glory is not fantastic meetings or a certain looking manifestation from God. The real glory, the one that exceeds all others, is Christ, the glorified One, the risen One, the all powerful One, the One now seated in glory. He is not just seated in heaven but seated "in" the glory. He is in the midst because His presence sustains the glory around Him. He is the center of the glory, the one manifesting it, allowing its beam of majesty to burst forth into the earth and touch lives.

You see, the glory is not for our entertainment or to say we have reached a bench mark of achievement. It is for us to be transformed and changed. It is for us to climb to higher realms of God and ascend His **Isaiah 2:2-3** mountain. That mountain is what God is building. He is not repeating past patterns or models but is building a new single corporate man breathing His life flow.

2 Corinthians 3:18 *"But we all, with open face beholding as in a glass the glory of the Lord, are changed into the same image from glory to glory, even as by the Spirit of the Lord."*

Moses' tabernacle, David's tabernacle, Solomon's temple, Zerubbabel's temple, and Herod the Great's temple, all had a fading glory... types of shadows of glory but not sustained. Just as much as each experienced degrees of God, they all fought breaches as well. They were times and seasons of dis-focus that caused idolatry to emerge. Today our dis-focus has created idols. We idolize certain leaders and believe they are infallible, thus making them a god. We idolize certain truths and set them above all other truths making them forms of false doctrine. We even take things once truly holy and made them common, thus making them unclean. Our iniquity has made us take our techniques and form them as doctrine. But God is bring us back to the original intention of His heart, relationship with Him above anything we can build. This relationship is Presence driven and focused. It is not how we do things but whether His breath is in the things we do. How then shall we bring back the ark of God into our midst?

The same question has been raised time and time again in the history of God's people. Men searched out the records of Church history and tried to duplicate a method that seemed to work. We seek all kinds of gimmicks that really require no sacrificial lifestyle on our part, all the while expecting God to stamp "approved" on our efforts. Nothing seems to work. It really comes down to a simple yet seldom heard message: a lifestyle of repentance.

Repentance is more than changing your mind because you got caught in wrongdoing. No!

The Breath of God

That kind of repentance is short lived and does not create lasting change. That type of repentance allows room for justification of actions and the ability to return to the wrongdoing. True heartfelt repentance is a brokenness that causes heart change. It is repentance that comes because the relationship with God is more valuable than the transgressions and iniquities we want to embrace. It is repentance that comes because we have broken the heart of God. This kind of lifestyle of repentance is what is needed to truly bring the ark of God back into the Church. David knew this and had to have deep heartfelt repentance before his second attempt to bring the ark. If we would do this, we would realize just how much we have to lay down our desires and thinking that we have the ways of God and come back to the due order He already has determined.

We know the intentions of God but we need to seek Him for the WAY the intention will be manifested. The ways of God are not beyond our reach, but they are beyond our natural understanding or process of reasoning. The ways of God always point to the ultimate conclusions and not the events along the journey. As we look at Jesus, the people were caught up in the daily life being portrayed and their benefit from it. God was more concerned about the Cross and the redemption it would bring to humanity and eventually to all creation.

Acts 15:16-17 *"After this I will return, and will build again the tabernacle of David, which is fallen down; and I will build again the ruins thereof, and I will set it up: That the residue of men might seek after the Lord, and all the Gentiles, upon whom my name is called, saith the Lord, who doeth all these things."*

The word "residue" here means '*those outcast or disregarded*'. This tells me that none of the models are truly the model God will build. Notice it says that God will build it, not us. We are not seeing the outcasts coming, being so drawn by our gatherings that they can't stay away. But what really is going to draw those so destitute or what will humble those so seemingly full of pride? It's the very nature of God! You see, the nature of God has all things within it. It has the gifts, it has the anointing, it has the power, but it also has HIM. The purest form of God! The nature confronts all things, establishes all things and releases all the possibilities of God for every situation.

After spending so many years in ministry and looking back, I can see that, at times, I also pursued all of these things thinking it would bring the move of God we needed. Maybe it would make me a better servant of God or help to convince the naysayers of the reality of the messages and even the existence of God. After years of pursuing and getting worn out in pursuit, wisdom began to settle in. In this season, I see only one ultimate goal and that is the pursuit of His presence. Nothing else matters and nothing else will satisfy. Everything else is lacking. So a 'letting go' must occur. As I have said many times, it's like climbing a ladder, you have to let go of the past rung to grab the one in the future above you. As good as all the things I have experienced and God has allowed me to see, there is still a desire for more. 'This can't be the end of what my life has held' is a thought I have constantly. I think deep down inside, all of us are in that same place of holy contentment but deep dissatisfaction at the same time. We know there is more; we just don't know exactly how to get there.

David, a man after God's own heart, also knew there was more. In his heart was a desire to build a dwelling place for God. But he also knew he needed that which held the Presence of God, the Ark of the Covenant, to be close to his life. As his first attempt failed and after heartfelt repentance occurred, David realized that he could not invent a "new cart" to carry the ark of His presence. It would require something from him. We too, must carry this upon the strength of our own backs and faith. A new cart does not require a holy priest to move it --- but an ark resting on the shoulders of a priest of God does. You see, what we are doing is trying to guide or steady the Presence but we are to CARRY IT! It is not about the strength of oxen carrying the Presence but the weakness of humanity.

David soon realized that a breach had occurred. It's pretty simple to know when God is not around any longer. It is like one man said to me years ago, "The Holy Spirit can leave months or even years before we notice". We think it just happened suddenly, but actually, the Holy Spirit was crowded out and no longer welcome! This is what has occurred today. We keep saying we have all of God when in reality; we are not willing to admit we let things slip. God can't give us something that we confess we already have. When we make an assumption of God's intentions, we step out of order.

1 Chron. 15:13 "The LORD our God made a breach upon us, for that we sought him not after the due order."

David realized a breach had occurred. It was not a breach in what they were doing in the tabernacle but a breach in relationship with God. The breach was not in the technique but in relationship. Today we have replaced relationship with techniques. The techniques have actually become idols to us as they have replaced relationship with the breath and nature of God.

The Davidical tabernacle that David set into motion would experience five distinct breaches over time:

1. Rebellion – Rehoboam's decision
   II Chronicles 10
   a. Israel's revolt
   b. Jeroboam rejects worship
   II Chronicles 11

      c. Revival under Jehoshaphat
      II Chronicles 17
2. Idols -- Ahaziah entertained them
II Chronicles 22
    a. Joash becomes king
    II Chronicles 23
    b. Repairs the temple, turns to idolatry
    II Chronicles 24
3. Idols to Baal by Ahaz
II Chronicles 28
    a. Judah invaded
    b. Cleansing of the temple
    II Chronicles 29
4. Idols by Manasseh
II Chronicles 33
    a. Josiah restored
    b. Temple repaired
    II Chronicles 34
5. Idols by Zedekiah, 70 years of Babylonian captivity
    a. Cyrus, King of Persia restored
    II Chronicles 36
    b. Based on prophetic words of Nehemiah and Ezra

As good as David's tabernacle was, after each breach occurred, the glory and presence of God it once held was never restored to the fullness prior to its breach. The people just didn't value what once was. We don't imitate past patterns but we do pursue past principles. We don't cherish the outcomes as much as the One who brings the outcomes.

We must recognize when something from a past order has served its purpose and its purpose is fulfilled. Copying the pattern does not make it have purpose again! It is just like truth. We need to know what truth God is emphasizing in this hour. It does not mean past truths are wrong, but they may not be what are needed for the moment of time we are in to bring the intentions of God to the earth.

The problem is we look at functions and believe functions are the answer when it is motive and intentions of the heart.

The rebuilding of the Tabernacle is:

1. The rebuilding of a royal priesthood
2. The ruling of kings
3. The release of Melchisedec order
4. Message of repentance that ushers in the Kingdom (not worship ushering in the Presence)

5. It is the coming forth and enlargement of a singular corporate man.
6. The breath and nature of God being at center stage in all that unfolds and is spoken
7. It is not past techniques or copied patterns.

This tabernacle will not just suddenly burst forth upon the earth in a blaze of glory, but will grow and grow and grow... it will be an eternal tabernacle and will continue to unfold until all men know of the "knowledge" of the glory of God. Now that will be attractive and that will be what men will desire to run into! That will also require for a people to be carriers of God's nature and God's breath. When they speak, life is released and that which is creative is put into motion.

There is another little known temple that God showed He desired to build... Ezekiel's temple.

Ezekiel 43:10-11 *"Thou son of man, shew the house to the house of Israel, that they may be ashamed of their iniquities: <u>and let them measure the pattern</u>. And if they be ashamed of all that they have done, shew them the form of the house, and the*

fashion thereof, and the goings out thereof, and the comings in thereof."
The vision of Ezekiel was the revealing of a pattern that God had intended to see completed. But this pattern was never built. Nor did God ever promise it would be, unless there was genuine national repentance and a turning toward God by the sinful nation. God's promise was conditional. Ezekiel's writings show how the glory of God surely, but reluctantly, withdrew from His habitation and returned to His place in the heavens. Yet in and through it all, He gave us a promise that He would return in the fullness of time, take up His habitation in a new Temple not made with the hands of men, and send forth a River of Life that would bring healing to the nations.

But first, Ezekiel must see the glory of God, and literally "eat the book". The Word must become a vital part of his very being before he could bring forth a clear and meaningful Word to the people of God. He must move in total union with God and his words must contain the breath of God. Since this pattern was never built but was part of the intention of God, perhaps it holds insights into what God is building in this hour.

Ezekiel 3:17 *"I have made thee a watchman unto the house of Israel: therefore hear the word at my mouth, and give them warning from me."*

Apostasy seems almost to have been the norm in the history of God's people. But, in every hour of abomination, God begins to prepare a remnant through whom He will fulfill His purposes, and bring a fresh thing into being. The first thing that occurs is Ezekiel has a visitation from God. He sees into the revelatory realm. He has a fresh encounter with the breath and nature of God. It will be required to face the apostasy all around him of idolatry and discontentment. This is why much injustice today is not being shifted. We have not taken the time for a fresh encounter with God's nature so His breath and words would be carried through and from us.

Ezekiel is told he is a watchman. He is given a sure identity from God. Then God's assignment is not all kinds of activity but a single activity. He is told to eat the book or scroll. By doing so, he sees the four faces of God, and he sees a wheel upon the earth... the wheel within the wheel. His entire being is saturated with God's nature. He has the nature of God's eyes, ears, voice and intentions. His own physical senses are inflamed by this fresh breath that has blown upon him. He is now ready to be God's instrument upon the earth.

Ezekiel 1:15 *"Behold one wheel upon the earth by the living creatures, with his four faces."*

He is seeing the motion of the Kingdom on the earth connected to the Kingdom of Heaven. Ezekiel was seeing four faces of God. The four dimensions of the Gospels. But he was also seeing them as a single corporate man or expression. These four faces would release four distinct breaths found in the rest of the book of Ezekiel as we read it. As these breaths are released, it will also release seven glories of God's intentions for the earth. These parallel the temple that God showed Ezekiel that he would build.

His Nature Formed - His Breath Released

Chapter 5

Four Breaths, Seven Glories

We are all looking for the next thing God is going to do. For some people, the latest program driven agenda is their focus. For others, the movement of the Spirit. We have signs and wonders seekers, glory manifestation addicts and past truth lovers. But does God have something He desires to build that has all the elements that draw man's attention and affections? Yes, he does!

Ezekiel saw something that was never built but God and the pattern seems to hold true to today. What everyone seems to have in common with all we seek after is that all things are connected to the nature of God. His nature is not only birthing all these dynamics but is also sustaining them. His nature always has His breath and His breath always desires to touch humanity.

In Ezekiel, there is a pattern that is present that I call the four breaths and the seven glories. It's amazing to study and see how the whole book unfolds with these dynamics and how parallel it is to our nation in the moment of time we are living. It is like a roadmap of our future now unfolding.

Just like the time of Ezekiel's writings, it appears we are also under a Babylonian system. We are held captive as the people of God by the circumstances and culture around us. We have promises and past heritage to draw from but still we seem to be somewhat paralyzed in advancing our cause of the Kingdom of God.

What God is building is a single corporate man that has the nature of God residing within and the breath of God will be released from that nature. Ezekiel saw God with four faces. He then experienced four distinct breaths coming from those faces. Those breaths had an effect on a nation held captive and upon the glory of God as well. They set God's glory in motion. Seven times the glory moves and brings those around it deeper in God. The four faces are the four Gospels of the nature of Christ. The seven glories are connected with the seven graces released from His nature found in **Isaiah 11:1-3**. The breaths bring the life that causes the glory to move, that releases His graces to come! This is how it unfolds:

1. The Glory with the Captivity

Ezekiel 3:12-13, 15 *"Then the Spirit took me up, and I heard behind me a voice of a great rushing, saying, Blessed be the glory of the LORD from his place. I heard also the noise of the wings of the living creatures that touched one another, and the noise of the wheels... then I came to them of the captivity."*

What we need is a fresh wind of the Spirit to blow upon us again. What we don't realize is the glory of God is already resting upon us even in our captivity. We are just not allowing God to take us from the place of sitting to be relocated where we begin to see the glory that is already resting upon us. You see, the Spirit or breath of God carried Ezekiel to the next place. God had a glory for those held captive. The glory resting upon them was not seen because of their lack of faith and spiritual dullness caused by the Babylonian culture surrounding them.

The one held captive was Judah. Judah represents praise, so praise was being held captive by the religious system but Glory was also resting on praise. This is still true today but also what is true is many have experienced this first breath and the praise and worship with the new song, created song, prophetic song, life-giving sound, is beginning to break forth and can't be held captive any longer!

But Ezekiel as God's messenger, was falling upon deaf ears. They just could not believe the depth of God in fullness. So Ezekiel sat down astonished with the other captives. He had nothing to say. He sat as though dumb for seven days, the number of God's completion and fullness. Unless God would speak, nothing he would say would be effective. He could speak words that were right and maybe even anointed, but he wanted more than that, he wanted words that carried the breath of God upon them. Words that would shift a nation. Then God spoke and gave him a commission and a mandate to be "a watchman unto the house of Israel." God's prophets must learn that they do not minister to the people because they are prophets. <u>They minister effectually only when God opens their mouth and gives them the Word from His heart that His people need.</u>

The current position of so many is of

watchmen in this hour. But this has its own dilemmas as well. Most are frustrated with the lack of so many things we see in the Body of Christ, leaders, and current structures. We are watching for God to build a people that will build His Kingdom. We have been honored with this position much like Ezekiel. We are watching for the life of God that flows at times for the moments it will be sustained.

The frustration we are experiencing is not seeing the Body functioning nor seeing the Church being effective in culture. We see the Church is confused in doctrine. It is not having everyone be like us. These are all effects of a far greater thing. The frustration that we as watchmen experience is seeing the lack of relationship with the Lord that causes a lack of spiritual life.

You see in this first breath and first glory that we are called to watch, not to build. In the next hour we will partner with Him in what HE WILL BUILD! Man does not build God's Church, but Jesus said He would build the Church and the gates of hell will not prevail against it. Hell has a legal right to prevail against what men build and call the Church.

In this hour, God is giving wisdom so we can be wise master builders of the Kingdom. What God is doing is preparing us and what we are doing is shaping His Church. This is why we feel frustration at not seeing what is called the Kingdom be in fullness. Men are wrestling with their wisdom being replaced with God's wisdom.

The Glory Resting Over Captivity

Ezekiel 3:23 *"Then I arose, and went forth into the plain: and, behold, the glory of the LORD stood there, as the glory which I saw by the river of Chebar."*

The breath carried Ezekiel into a place that probably was unihabitated, the plain. The level place. The place the glory was already waiting on him to answer the breaths beckoning to come. The glory, *Kabad*, "stood" = '*to stand or remain as for an appointed time*'. The glory was already there. He had to allow the breath to bring him to it. It is a glory that releases the original intention of God, which we are just now beginning to know God's intention. It is not a new glory but a glory that is already in place. It is not coming to us but we are repositioning to it.

The remnant is being trained to GO wherever He sends them. This is the training we have been under. It is also part of the structure God is building, not a physical structure but entirely spiritual. We have focused way too much on what is fleshly and not enough on what is eternal. Part of that structure will contain those who are captive by the Lord. There are so many that are not participating in this Glory while others are being drawn to God not knowing any reason why. For some, their captivity is being turned. Let me be clear, I am not talking about the captivity of the unsaved but the captivity of the saved!

Psalm 14:7 (KJV 1900) — 7 Oh that the salvation of Israel were come out of Zion! When the LORD bringeth back the captivity of his people, Jacob shall rejoice, and Israel shall be glad.

This glory is an ILLUMINATON GLORY. It is when the light of God shines in the hearts of men, **II Corinthians 4:6**. It is an awakening glory that asks "why sit we here until we die?" It brings revelation of the current word that sits before us. This is seen in the amount of revelation that is being released. It is required to shift us from captivity. It will start to move us to the plain, a new location. Some of the revelation still has a mixture, but some of it is beginning to take on a pure stream.

This first breath is required by everyone to go forward. Some have already experienced God illuminating their understanding and have decided to step out of the captivity that surrounds them. They have entered the second breath.

The Glory at the Inner Gate of the Temple

Ezekiel 8:3-4 *"And he put forth the form of an hand, and took me by a lock of mine head; and the Spirit lifted me up between the earth and the heaven, and brought me in the visions of God to Jerusalem, to the door of the inner gate that looketh toward the north; where was the seat of the image of jealousy, which provoketh to jealousy. And, behold, the glory of the God of Israel was there."*

Now the breath came again and instead of

The Breath of God

carrying him, it lifted him. It caused him to not rely on the breath to do all the effort but the breath is now the motivator. This breath lifts him and repositions him to be suspended between heaven and earth, the second heaven. This is the correct position for a child of God. We should be stewarding the second heaven, accessing the third heaven and implementing into the earth. (For more on this topic, see my book "*Stewarding the Second Heaven*".)
Not everything we see in second heaven is from God and there is something he now can see from the access point where the breath has taken him to. He is at the door of the gate. Doors represent hearts and gates represent entrances into cities. He is being brought to the heart of authority.

But he also sees the image of jealousy. The wording in Hebrew means 'the *idol of zeal, envy and wrong passions*'. He actually was seeing the place of authority had been allowed to rule over the city and the hearts of those who were there.

But another thing was also present: the Glory or *Kabod* of God. Wherever evil exists, God's glory is also present to be drawn upon. This glory is present even in the places of our structures where we have erected abominations ... the seat of the image of jealousy. It is a glory above the glory of man upon the earth.

He was taken from Babylon to Jerusalem. His captivity had changed and what held his attention was not the captivity of the Babylonian culture but was now Jerusalem, the city of peace. He was taken from worldly surroundings and taken to the north gate. The north gate was the one of four looking inward to the inner court of Solomon's temple. The Glory was at the entrance point of the structure.

This breath is a repositioning breath. It is a breath for entrance in. So will it be for what God is building, entrance points of the spiritual structure that have the *kabod* sitting upon them..... Kingdom centers... more than training but points of glory. This glory is being deposited in us at this hour. It is in our hearts but not fully deposited. It is a glory that rests between two realms, the earthy and the heavenly. It is a glory that draws men to enter and allows what is unclean to become clean. It is a glory that allows the mixture so the mixture can and will be removed. This is why leaders in this hour are still allowed to minister but yet are unholy. God will purge out the unholiness.

<u>This glory is a FREEDOM glory</u>. It holds deliverance, expressiveness, and outward manifestations because of inward transformation. I liken it to being born again, again. Now instead of deliverance from sin and a new found freedom, there is deep liberty because of the nature of God and His breath in our lives.

This glory happened when His people came to Him with empty hands to be filled with only what He gives us and nothing but that which comes from Him – and when we throw away our own idols and our desires for His liberty. We are seeing the beginning stages of this glory in the Church. Many are experiencing this in different degrees. Free flow gatherings, prophetic flow worship, it is beginning to come in Spirit driven teaching.

Then the Lord took Ezekiel on a tour of the Temple area and showed him **all the**

<u>abominations that were being perpetrated by an apostate priesthood.</u> There were creeping things in the house of God:

- **abominable beasts**...
- **Idols** portrayed upon the wall...
- the leader of the **elders offering incense to false Gods**...
- women at one of the gates **weeping over a heathen God** (Tammuz) who was believed to have died; they were in mourning because of this...
- **men worshipping the sun** in the location of the brazen sea (between the porch and the altar),where God had intended a washing and a cleansing of His people.

Beloved, there are a lot of creeping things in the House of God today. I have heard of so many things that have gone on or have been allowed. And we wonder why we have lost our

The Breath of God

voice to a nation. There are going to be some strong words against it by His servants who have His nature and carry His breath. These words will not just be simple rebukes or even strong teaching but will release depths of holiness that men's hearts will faint and deep repentance will be demanded and felt.

The greatest admonition is the false doctrine, positions, and authority being exercised. These are the things that lead people astray by the multitudes and also make the Church look foolish to the world. The greatest idol we have is a leadership idol. We have made leaders into idols and some leaders have made themselves to be idolized! This has made us lose our relationship with God as we live our lives through the lives of leaders who have become our way to God and our superstars.

We will see order come back in doctrine and we will see a new breed of leader rise who will not only confront all things by words filled with God's breath but also by the nature of holiness becoming the standard.

These two areas of admonition and idols is what is holding freedom and liberty from so many and keeping them bound. But in this hour, there are those whose lives have come through the flame and are hidden in Christ. Those who are desiring but one thing and it is Him in purest form and extreme nature. They have had the second breath, the breath of freedom and will not let any admonition or idol steal the freedom from their life.

The Glory Moves To The Door Of The House

The first and second glories are now, at the time of this writing, moving in the Church. The breath has come but for some it will take more time to receive the breath of God. Old models and mindsets are trapping us in forms of captivity. Wrong and misinterpreted doctrines and leadership unwilling to engage in what God is currently doing, due to the fact of their position being threatened, are hindering the forward moment of a corporate body moving as one. Yet in the midst of it all, God has a plan unfolding to build what He has determined and it will be full of His glory and all men will have knowledge of it.

Ezekiel 9:3 *"And the glory of the God of Israel was gone up from the cherub, whereupon he was, to the threshold of the house."*

The glory was sitting over the captivity and also sitting at the door and gate and now the glory is taking us deeper. It has moved and brought us to the threshold of the house, the entrance point of true encounters. This is a glory of entrance. A glory that requires sanctification, a setting apart, an undivided heart. We can no longer have the mixture that has been allowed that has caused us to be unclean. We no longer can be halted between two opinions. If He is God, then we must serve Him with our whole heart. The stony heart must go for us to continue moving with His glory.

This Glory resting at the threshold is safe guarding the treasures of God from wandering eyes and hearts who desire the deep things of God but only to spend them on their own foolishness. This Glory is an HONORING glory!

It will require us to be marked by God and set

apart. Not marked by the abominations. For many it will require a rethinking of doctrinal stances. For others, a shifting of what was thought to be truth. Still others will face a total abandonment of institutionalized beliefs formed by men.

Ezekiel 9:4 *"mark upon the foreheads of the men that sigh and that cry for all the abominations that be done in the midst thereof."*
Many want to walk with him but don't want to pay the full price of true discipleship. Most today are living as priests of Levi. They are in bondage to rules and laws and regulations. Even in the full Gospel or apostolic camp. It is a fear not faith motivation.

The marking of God is the survival of the testing we have gone through that reveals our real motives. Like Christ, we must have the scars. Without the wrestling with God, our motives will not be pure. But the wrestling will bring an even far greater weight of His glory upon us. This makes us of 'like precious faith'. This is what forms the army of God. This is what creates us being in oneness of **John 17**. It is not deciding to believe but all having the same nature, the nature of Christ truly formed within us. This is what makes us be in covenant with each other that is deeper than all the covenant agreements we have written and signed as a show of good faith. This is covenant written upon our hearts towards each other. A covenant that says 'what I do towards you I am doing towards the nature of Christ in you'. I know what that is because that same nature is living in me as well. A new priesthood will emerge, the Melchizedek Priesthood, who will walk in the face of His glory!

Many are called but few are chosen (the hand picking of God) to not just bear His name but His nature. You have been chosen to be marked not by some false demonic mark that imitates. You have been marked by God and sealed as His chosen!

The reason we have wrestled with doctrine is to know the character and nature of God. Those that have shifted doctrinally for the worse are reluctant to truly know God. Those who have shifted doctrinally have shifted because they have seen that it wasn't their doctrine that convinced them but the character behind the doctrine! It is not to know the promise of God, but to know God, Who is our promise!

It is an <u>HONORING GLORY</u> --- His character. God bestows honor not on our actions but on our character. He can fully honor us because His nature is within. He is not just approving us but Himself within us. Now that makes it easy to die to self, doesn't it? It makes a desire that our life would truly be pleasing in Him and the more of Him living in me, the more pleasing I am to Him!

Romans 8:18 (KJV 1900) — *18 For I reckon that the sufferings of this present time are not worthy to be compared with the glory which shall be revealed in us.*

It's amazing that we suffer so many things, some self induced. I tell people, if you're going to suffer, then suffer for righteousness sake. Suffer- not to go out and function in spiritual things or Christian work. But suffer that Christ would be formed in you. Wrestle with yourself. Wrestle with your sin. Deny not only that which is evil but even that which is good and appears harmless, if it is distracting you from Christ. Now that is suffering!

God spoke to me years ago that He wanted my

Saturdays. So for over ten years I gave Him the entire day. I studied, prayed, worshipped and sought Him. While others were out enjoying the sunny day or watching the game, or doing whatever, I was in my office seeking Him. At times, I looked at it as suffering, but then when I realized what His true suffering really was, I knew I had not suffered, but had been given a privilege. It formed the nature within. It made me a revelatory teacher. I had been given a special place before God. I do not regret those Saturdays.

God said to Ezekiel, ***"The iniquity of the house of Israel and Judah is exceeding great, and the land is full of blood, and the city full of perverseness: for they say, The LORD hath forsaken the earth, and the LORD seeth not." (Ezekiel 9:9)***

God always preserves for Himself a faithful remnant, no matter how great are the abominations. And God will spare them in the day of His wrath. God will spare our nation as well as the remnant. He is pressing into allowing the nature to be formed in us.

Just as the glory has moved again, we begin to

see the glory is always transient, always in motion, always seemingly on an assignment. It is a glory that is like heaven coming to earth. As all of heaven is in motion, so this glory is as well.

It will come to the door of the house. Right now there are some being positioned for the glory to enter the house as they are opening the door. These are structures, spiritual structures that are becoming entrance points. These points of entrance will protect the glory and what is most precious, God will put inside His house. They are the new look of the Church's expression beginning to emerge. Apostolic churches and gatherings, and Kingdom centers emerging. Also, some of the Houses of Prayer, if they are not just focused on one truth and are truly balanced in Kingdom premise. All are allowing God to work a deep process within them. It is a process that creates His nature and embraces His breath.

You can recognize these places because the message is uncompromising. It is filled with truth and the atmosphere holds tremendous freedom and liberty. These are places seeking to establish true holiness and not forms of it. Places where the people embrace God's sanctification, separation and even drawing away from worldliness. Though small in number, they are steadily growing with others coming for "reality" that they find missing in other settings.

I see so many disillusioned in the Church and also with the Church. Many have become prodigals or have been disjointed because of not fitting. They were waiting for this which is coming and even now is. For some, they drew into home settings wanting more accountability and greater community. Many of these settings will also hear the call to come and be part of the corporate man being formed.

The Glory Fills The Court to the point of touching the Cherubim

Ezekiel 10:4 *"Then the glory of the LORD went up from the cherub, and stood over the threshold of the house; and the house was filled with the cloud, and the court was full of the brightness of the LORD's glory."*

His Nature Formed - His Breath Released

Once we have decided the glory is greater than my captivity and we have allowed it to illuminate us, it brings us freedom so we truly desire sanctification and being set aside. We then are in the right position to be filled with His nature to a new capacity.

Now when we begin to be filled, a shifting occurs. It is not so much a thing of being thrilled with His glory as we begin to truly feel the weight of it pressing upon us. It is the weightiness of His presence we are being asked to carry. It is like a mantle we are to carry. It is the same glory that Jesus carried. It is Joseph's coat of many colors showing the different dynamics of God's nature. It is a glory that touches both heaven and earth. The glory stands still so we can be filled. It does not come and go but remains until the brightness fills the court, the holy place of our lives.

This is the most precious element that God is putting into the house He is building now. Just as all the things up to this moment have been outside, now we begin to see the structure will contain a greater glory of filling. It says it was full. This is a statement of fact speaking forth the degree of God's intention. For it to be filled will also require the fullness of the illumination of all hidden things. Darkness cannot be here. Hence the process we have gone through to allow His glory to come.

I believe for the most part, we are waiting to deal with things in our lives believing things like "where God is, sickness cannot exist, God's holiness is greater than my sin" and other concepts. We believe when His glory comes, then we will deal with our sin. But as we look at scriptures, we see that God's glory came because of man's separation first. Yes, people saw His glory from afar and repented, but they could not participate in it until their heart was pure. We, for the most part, are waiting, waiting for the outbreak of God to get right, waiting for the move to come and then prepare. Waiting for "that service" thinking then it will change me. But God can't fill a vessel that is already full. We have to empty ourselves!

The "Court" will be filled, yes we can interpret it as our court, but we can also see it to mean the Glory of Government and Justice, Courts of Heaven upon the Earth. As a nation is crying out for injustice to be shifted, it will not happen by simply changing laws and bringing forced reformation. It will only come by changing the moral compass and culture expression of morality. It will only come by a move of God, but that move has to be something so deep it confronts the moral indifferences we experience today. When the Church becomes full of God's nature and full of His glory so that men are without excuse and their hearts are constantly confronted, they, too will cry out and ask "what must we do to be saved?"

I had a vision years ago of the final outpouring, the final movement of God upon the earth. I had probably no less than twenty of these. In this vision, we were sitting in a building having a meeting. We were all singing but it seemed no one was leading. People had come to spend every free moment before the Lord. Some were dirty, others were clean, but all were seeking with what appeared to be the exact same hearts and passions.

I could see people praying and healing being released while we all sang. I also saw prophetic words being released. In another area, there was deliverance and it seemed we were all being preached to at the same time, not by a man but by the voice of the Holy Spirit.

I was led to leave the service and go outside and I met a person walking by. I simply came up to them and the nature of God was so upon me that they were compelled to turn into the meeting. As they went down the side aisle looking for a place to sit, it was as if a shepherd's hook grabbed their neck and violently pulled them to the front. They dropped to their knees and cried out to God for mercy with repentance and were saved and filled with the Holy Spirit and began to speak in tongues. All of this was going on at the same time. The Lord spoke to me and said *"When I come in this next move, you will know for no man will need to preach or convince but My presence alone will draw and woo and convict and preach and do all things through you without you saying a single word."*

There is a sound associated with this glory. It is as if His breath has formed a sound at this point. A sound that is heard in the spirit realm. A sound that draws men. The sound of His glory reverberated throughout the whole

Temple, even to the outer court. And when this happens, His Word will go forth "even to the outer court."

1 Corinthians 2:9–10 (KJV 1900) — 9 *But as it is written, Eye hath not seen, nor ear heard, neither have entered into the heart of man, the things which God hath prepared for them that love him. 10 But God hath revealed them unto us by his Spirit: for the Spirit searcheth all things, yea, the deep things of God.*

1 Corinthians 1:29–2:5 (KJV 1900) — 29 *That no flesh should glory in his presence. 30 But of him are ye in Christ Jesus, who of God is made unto us wisdom, and righteousness, and sanctification, and redemption: 31 That, according as it is written, He that glorieth, let him glory in the Lord. 1 And I, brethren, when I came to you, came not with excellency of speech or of wisdom, declaring unto you the testimony of God. 2 For I determined not to know any thing among you, save Jesus Christ, and him crucified. 3 And I was with you in weakness, and in fear, and in much trembling. 4 And my speech and my preaching was not with enticing words of man's wisdom, but in*

demonstration of the Spirit and of power: 5 That your faith should not stand in the wisdom of men, but in the power of God.

Paul was stating he was ministering out of the glory residing within Him. It was more than substance or promises, or anointing or past knowledge of God, or truths in which he had gotten a firm grip. It was coming from the nature, the character, the glory. It was from the well that never would run dry. The place of "Living" waters. <u>This is His FILLING GLORY --- HIS Presence .</u> This is what we are all waiting for!

When His Glory comes to His people, it will mean cleansing and purifying for the people of God who submit to His dealings… but it will not change the rebellious and obstinate of heart. God is looking for the ones who give their lives as a free will offering to the Lord and like Isaiah said, "Here am I, send me." With the people now in the right place, now God will turn to discipling the nations.

The Glory Moves To The Eastern Gate

Ezekiel 10:18-19 *"Then the glory of the LORD departed from off the threshold of the house, and stood over the cherubim... the wheels also were beside them, and every one stood at the door of the east gate of the LORD's house; and the glory of the God of Israel was over them above."*

As heaven was touched, so now Earth will be touched. God's presence will come not just into their lives but into their land. Ezekiel spoke about the impending judgments coming to them as a nation. As Ezekiel prophesied to them, one of the princes of the people fell down dead. When the prince of the people fell down dead, Ezekiel fell on his face before God and cried aloud for God to have mercy upon them as a people. We are not at this point in God's timetable but it is coming. The presence of God will demand holiness from the least to the greatest.

When the Glory of God returns to His people,

we are going to witness some very severe judgments. We all know the story of Ananias and Sapphira in **Acts 5**. They held back part of the price of some land they had sold and lied about it. For them to sell a portion and give was really no hardship, just an adjustment in lifestyle. In **Acts 4**, we see a great grace was upon them all, not just the disciples but every believer. They were living in the nature and breath of God as He provided for every need. Healings and miracles were occurring. People were living in an ongoing metamorphism or changing manner of life, and not just experiencing grace or change occasionally. People were ministering to each other's needs.

You see, they had all things common. The selling of needs and re-distributing had nothing to do with balancing a social system or economic structure. The word 'common' can mean *'two people having a common interest'* or *'agreement concerning an idea'*. But when you really study this out, it means that each person had a distinct call and relationship with God and that all believers shared this same calling of service and relationship with God. The selling of property and distribution made was to eliminate the physical distractions and excuses so they could concentrate on fulfilling the call and service for God. Since all had this and understood the importance of it, everyone was willing to participate because He was close to their own hearts.

When Ananias and Sapphira lied to the Holy Spirit, they were basically saying in their heart, that fulfilling the call of God that each believer had was not important, that God cannot meet our needs so we have to hold back to do it ourselves. In essence, they were directly coming against the grace of God resting and operating in the Church. The impact of their action must have been far reaching because we go from chapter four where all needs were being met because of people functioning in their calling, to chapter six needing a man full of faith to believe for the needs to be met as they were lacking. The apostles had moved in chapter four to being released to prayer and study and by chapter six, they were reduced to waiting tables and trying to meet needs. The only thing sitting in between, in chapter 5, is Ananias and Sapphira.

I have found myself many times in this same situation. I end up doing physical things because someone else is unwilling to do them. When this occurs, the ministry seems to slow down. It is like taking the coach of a team and telling them to go clean the showers in the locker room. The game goes on and everyone still gets to play but the strategy gets suspended. I can tell you from personal experience and from talking to many leaders that it is one way to devalue a leader's role and make them lose heart quickly. They will do the work without complaint because of the servant attitude within them, even though others do not see what is going on. A leader knows that all the jobs have to be done no matter what. So they eliminate each one needing done and then come back to what their real responsibility is. I summarize it this way: you can't take the senior man and reduce him to the lowest role and expect the ministry to advance at the highest rate. A man told me to stop doing announcements. He said it's like you got this great pitch hitter whose going to get up and speak and before you can see what he has to offer, you have him cleaning the gear. You have devalued him.

It was not Peter that killed Ananias and Sapphira. It was the nature of God within him releasing the breath of God upon them. They had refused change and refused to embrace the great grace that had come. I imagine this great grace is something we have never experienced or even know how to comprehend. It had to be part of some of the greatest dynamics of God ever seen.

God could not let their actions as influential people go untouched. The whole community knew who they were and they probably were ones with great influence upon people. They had determined to have a head on disagreement with God's actions and intentions. In many ways, they were actually defiant. But what they did not know is the Presence and Glory then resting on the temple had come to cleanse the temple. When we don't deal with the things in our hearts, the cleansing can sometimes be extremely severe. This was the glory of God that was in their midst both cleansing and judging His Temple. Immediately after the story of their death a verse jumps out of the scriptures: "***no man durst join himself***" to this company of believers, because of the fear of God in their midst.
This glory will cause a real dividing. It will

cause all people to know all about it and will stay away, unless they are prepared to come face-to-face with God in His holy Temple. This is a DIVIDING Glory --- holiness & sanctification.

As this glory comes and begins to divide, it will begin to set aside a nation! This is the glory that will bring a national purging that is so desperately needed. It is a glory that is not for our name's sake but God defending His name Himself. This is a glory resting in and upon His house that causes the nation to take notice!

The Glory Moves To The Mountain On The East

Ezekiel 11:1 (KJV 1900) — *1 Moreover the spirit lifted me up, and brought me unto the east gate of the LORD's house, which looketh eastward: and behold at the door of the gate five and twenty men; among whom I saw Jaazaniah the son of Azur, and Pelatiah the son of Benaiah, princes of the people.*

The Spirit --- the breath --- *ruwach* of God lifts him again. We are now at the third breath.

You see, where the glory is, is where we are led to go and now it is resting at the Eastern gate. This is the place the *Ecclesia* is to function. It is the place that laws are made that govern. It also is the place of opening into a city. Those gathered there determined whether to allow or NOT allow someone into their city through the gate.

But sitting in this place were evil men. They had been allowed to occupy because the true *Ecclesia* had not taken their place. They had made wrong choices and allowed much evil within their city. But now God's glory moved in and along with it, the true *Ecclesia* had come.

You see God established government and government is always in place. If the Church or *Ecclesia* doesn't want to govern, then satanic and evil government will step in and take its place. Unless the Church comes and begin to truly govern from a place of real strength, we won't see reformation take hold in fullness. The place of truly governing is not from concepts of God but from the nature of God. When the earth is governed from that perspective, it will begin to take on the dynamics of Heaven of the government of God that is established there.

This is the Kingdom established and the positioning for redeeming the earth. It is the place of being ready to represent a Kingdom to the Father and a Church without spot or blemish. The Church without spot is us individually but also us corporately. The corporate way we govern is making righteous judgments. We are concerned about judging others. This comes because we are concerned about judging from our nature. But once the nature of Christ is fully formed in us, then righteous judgments will come. Christ made what we would look at as many judgmental statements, but He judged from an established righteous nature. This kind of rightly dividing will cause fear and reverence to once again come to God's people and to those who don't yet believe.

Ezekiel 11:23 *"And the glory of the LORD went up from the midst of the city, and stood upon the mountain which is on the east side of the city"*

This Glory rests upon the mountain of the

Lord, resting upon what He has built. It will move from the covering of the city to a higher place, the covering of the mountain. The advantage point. The place alliances are formed and covenants are struck. It will move to look down upon what has been allowed. It rests upon what He has built.

Isaiah 2:1-4 (KJV 1900) — *1 The word that Isaiah the son of Amoz saw concerning Judah and Jerusalem. 2 And it shall come to pass in the last days, That the mountain of the Lord's house shall be established in the top of the mountains, And shall be exalted above the hills; And all nations shall flow unto it. 3 And many people shall go and say, Come ye, and let us go up to the mountain of the Lord, To the house of the God of Jacob; And he will teach us of his ways, And we will walk in his paths: For out of Zion shall go forth the law, And the word of the Lord from Jerusalem. 4 And he shall judge among the nations, And shall rebuke many people: And they shall beat their swords into plowshares, And their spears into pruninghooks: Nation shall not lift up sword against nation, Neither shall they learn war any more.*

The Breath of God

We will deeply learn of His ways and really walk in His paths. For the most part, we really don't know the ways of God or the "how" God works out the things that concern us. If we did, we would not be in panic, fear, unbelief, depression, anxiousness or all the other things we deal with. The ways of God are higher than our ways and with the glory now resting above the city and upon the mountain- yes, God is showing this.

We also struggle to walk in His paths. We walk in His truth. We walk in His precepts. But walking in His "path" is a very different thing. The word 'path' means '*the way or manner of life*'. It comes from a word that means '*to journey as a traveler with or without a company of people*'. For me to walk in the path of God means I am allowing His nature to so dictate my life that what I do and where I go are the places He has gone before me and taken every stone of stumbling out of the way. It is as if I am walking in the steps of God of where He has been.

This verse in **Isaiah 2** holds much promise for me personally. In the 1850's, a group of men called the Iowa Band came to our state. They were commissioned and sent by Charles

Finney from his church in Oberlin, Ohio, with a mandate to build the *Isaiah 2* mountain of the Lord in Iowa. Over time, they established the first colleges and had over 250 Sunday Schools throughout the state teaching the same thing. Their network of circuit riders trained over 10,000 ministers and sent them further West to establish the Kingdom of God as the nation was developing. But for many reasons, they did not complete their assignment in fullness and since then, God has endeavored to bring this to light so others can run with this vision. In studying the spiritual history of our state, I see how this mountain is being established.

This glory is a covenantal alignment glory. It will bring the oneness Jesus talked about in **John 17**. This is a single expression of the corporate man being seen, a coming together with a purpose so far greater than just unity. Unity among leaders is nothing but a false finish line and is easily attained. Webster's defines it as: *the quality or state of not being multiple, a condition of harmony, the quality or state of being made one, a totality of related parts.* For the most part, it simply means we have decided to agree. Unity can be based on not agreeing for the sake of coming together, or compromising what you believe to create unity. In the past, what I have seen is unity is generally accomplished by the setting of the lowest common denominator that can be agreed to.

But in the case of oneness being seen that Jesus talked about in ***John 17***, it is much different. He said we would be <u>one</u> in four areas, in the Word, the Name, the glory and perfection. Agreeing upon these things is not the same as being <u>one</u> in these things. Paul said it again in ***Ephesians 4:1-6***. He states that unity from the Spirit or the nature of Christ is what keeps peace. You could also state that if there is not peace among us then we are not allowing the nature to be formed in us. He then states seven things concerning being <u>one</u> Body: one Spirit, one hope, one Lord, one faith and baptism and God, who is above all, through all and in all. Paul was again stating the nature is the key to bring us into oneness and not just deciding to agree. If that was the case, then we are in unity with demons because they even agreed, recognized the Christ in Paul and cried out announcing it.

It is being in harmony not with each other, but with Christ and purposes of Christ upon the earth. You see, we have missed the point and left Christ out of the standard of unity and made ourselves and agendas the focal point. We gather and have so many meetings trying to establish something in our human effort that only God can do by His Spirit. The desire for us to be connected is what is always in the back of our minds. It is a desire that God placed there. We must have patience until Christ is formed in us and then allow His spirit to connect us with those of like precious faith. Not everyone will come into oneness, since not all will allow Christ to be formed to that degree.

But when we finally do understand His ways and walk in His paths, we will see ourselves put the childishness of our agendas aside and walk in a company made in His likeness so much we all appear the same. Now that is oneness! Unity will never make us look that way.

During this time, we will also see the great army of **Ezekiel 37** being formed. It is an army not slain by battle but an army that is lifeless because of the lack of sustained life coming to them, hence they are in a dry place and in a valley. The valley is where battles were fought.

The Breath of God

An army that has come to the end of itself.

The role of those who have been in the process of the nature of God formed in them will be given a command to prophesy. Just like **Rev. 11:11** again. The word 'again' means *anew*. A new way of prophesying, not just fore-telling but speaking and creating. The bones are commanded to "Hear the Word" of the Lord. This is the oneness of the word in **John 17**. It is not just any type of word or prophecy. But a word of coming together. This is what is needed. A God breathed word coming from the nature of God. This is the only kind of word from God that will cause us to come together. That's the sound from heaven that I am desiring to rally around.

This God breathed word will produce a noise, a shaking, and a coming together. It will cause a certain type of hearing. The word 'hearing' in **verse 4** means *'to hear with obedience, understanding, to proclaim, to hear with interest and attentiveness'*. Only a God breathed word will cause this kind of response.

The noise is not the noise of coming together but the word 'noise' means *'a thundering proclamation'*. It is a word meaning *'a voice'*. It is used when someone is calling aloud to someone else. The voice of God coming with His breath with thundering invitation. Booming so loudly that all hear it even those that are dead!

It will cause a shaking indeed. 'Shaking' means *'an earthquake, a rushing, a quivering, a trembling'*. This is more than some old bones rattling around. This is something that causes the whole earth to begin to tremble at His word. It causes men's hearts to almost fail them. It causes and demands a response because the creative force of God's voice is in play upon the earth again!

The outcome is the coming together bone to bone. The word 'bone' means *'body and the word coming togethe*r' means *'to draw close'* or *'to approach'*. So bodies will come together and approach each other. Together they will approach this sound that the voice released. The word has emphasis of coming together to be presented! Presented to receive His breath of life to enter.

This process must happen before the breath of

The Breath of God

God can enter into a corporate man to rise up. We are sitting right now with the noise and it's shaking but we have not yet come together. The shaking process has been going on now for some time. I believe it is because we've not heard a true God breathed word from heaven to rally around and the shaking is not a rushing or quivering before God but rather a shaking of our doctrines and manmade structures which is very different. The real shaking has not yet occurred because we have not yet had the God breathed voice released!

But just like this army in Ezekiel is seen as coming together, there still was not life in them until the breath came. This breath in ***Ezekiel 37*** is the sixth breath that we have been talking about, found in the sixth Glory forming a corporate man.

Ezekiel is commanded in **verse nine** to prophesy to the four winds. It is the four Gospels, the four faces of God, and the four winds of God coming as a single breath coming to blow into this army to cause it to rise up. You see only God's nature and breath will cause us to come to the position we truly are to be in. We will not just rise up in typical fashion but will rise as an exceeding great army. The restoration of hope will return anew to so many who are believers and leaders worn out from the life of ministry. They will be infused again with the vigor of youthful salvation mingled with the wisdom of life experience. This exceeding great army will march across the land as a single corporate expression of the Christ upon the earth. They will have nothing to prove but to show forth His glory!

Just how great will this army be? It will have died to self and selfish agendas. It will have heard a sound and voice and responded. It will have the breath and nature of God flowing within. In **Ezekiel 37:14** it is spelled out pretty clearly, "*(I) shall put my spirit in you, and ye shall live, and I shall place you in your own land: then shall ye know that I the Lord have spoken it, and performed it, saith the Lord.*"

The Glory Fills the House He has built and He is now in the House!

Ezekiel 43:5–7 (KJV 1900) — *5 So the spirit took me up, and brought me into the inner* *court; and, behold, the glory of the LORD filled the house. 6 And I heard him speaking unto me out of the house; and the man stood by me. 7 And he said unto me, Son of man, the place of my throne, and the place of the soles of my feet, where I will dwell in the midst of the children of Israel for ever, and my holy name, shall the house of Israel no more defile, neither they, nor their kings, by their whoredom, nor by the carcases of their kings in their high places.*

The fourth breath has come and the corporate man is formed. God is dwelling in the house He has built, not made with human hands. This is where we walk before His face in glory like Moses did, David did, Paul did, etc. His throne has been established and He is both dwelling and ruling from the position of His authority.

This is where shadows bring healing because of Presence. This is the place people experience conviction of sin because of His holiness. This is the place hearts are confronted because of His justice. I put it this way: it is as if the throne of heaven and all its authority and grace has come down to the earth to rule in such a manner that the earth will be redeemed. This is TRANSPARENT glory or transcended glory.

We become a doorway to heaven as Melchisedec kings and priests upon the earth. We know how to access heaven and know how to implement heaven's intentions into the earth. We are living our lives transparently. They no longer see us but truly do see Him living in us. It is as if they peer into us, they see heaven because of our transparency. We become like an open door that John saw in **Revelation 4**. We become an entrance point for others to experience Him in all His glory and authority. The early apostles went through the process and when people saw them, they saw Christ. When they saw them, they understood heaven. When they saw them, it was as if they had peered into the eyes of God living in them. This is when our footsteps leave a trail of His kingdom!

RIVERS OF WATER FROM THIS TEMPLE WILL FLOW

The seven glories will be the fullness of Christ coming upon His bride. It will be like a mantle that we will wear as many faceted colors and expressions like Joseph's coat of many colors. This will be an outward shining forth of the Glory of God because of an inward work that has been completed. This is the position to close the current age as we know it and bring forth the Kingdom age on the earth.

The earth is groaning for the manifestation of the sons of God of **Romans 8:18-23,** who will touch all of humanity. As we, the children of God, have taken on the nature of the Christ and are carriers of His breath, we then will be positioned to redeem the earth in fullness. We will usher in the things described in Thessalonians and Revelation, and "***the knowledge of the glory of the Lord will cover the earth as the waters cover the sea***" (**Habakkuk 2:14**).

Then we will see the fulfillment of Ezekiel 47. The river of God will flow and a healing of the nations will come in fullness. The waters that brought forth out of the right side of ***Ezekiel 47:2***, as the waters ran out of the side of Jesus when He was on the cross and was pierced with the sword. It will come into this river along with others to the ankle, knee, and loins. The word 'ankle' means '*to cease, finality, to come to an end*'. It is symbolic of Passover.

We will come to 'the knee' which means

'blessing, praise, and to kneel down and reverence'. It is symbolic of Pentecost. We'll also come to the point of our loins. The word 'loins' means *'a readiness for service'* and is symbolic of the tabernacle. The river of God's Glory rises, built by the return as **verse 6** says to the "brink" of the river. The word 'brink' means *'speech or language'*. We will be saying the same things that God is saying in heaven. As the trees gathered at the brink, or the language of heaven, we are today along with a multitude of people, gathered at the banks of God and we are waiting for someone to go in. For someone to test the stream of God's glory. But who will be worthy for this to occur and enter into what is descending from heaven? It will be those who have desired to peer into the hidden things. Those who would carry His presence like Charles Finney, that when he was put upon a train, all on the train would feel the presence of God- bringing repentance. The nation shall be healed and the land will be inherited. All will know the presence of God is indeed amongst and in His people with great breath and force. The end of the age will come and the eternal age will begin to break forth.

Chapter 6

Four Breaths Seven Glories Overview

1. The Glory With The Captivity

>This is an ILLUMINATON <u>GLORY</u>
>Light in the hearts 2 Cor. 4:6 --
>REVELATION OF WORD

Ezek. 3:12-13, 15 *"Then the Spirit took me up, and I heard behind me a voice of a great rushing, saying, Blessed be the glory of the LORD from his place. I heard also the noise of the wings of the living creatures that touched one another, and the noise of the wheels... then I came to them of the captivity."*

The "Spirit" – RUWACH -- THE BREATH OF GOD carried him to the place where the glory was.

The frustration a watchman experiences is seeing the lack of relationship with the Lord that causes a lack of spiritual life.

ACTS outpouring in upper room-**Acts 2:1**

2. The Glory At The Inner Gate Of The Temple

It is a <u>FREEDOM glory</u> -- deliverance, expressiveness, outward because of inward work.

Ezekiel 8:3-4 *"And he put forth the form of an hand, and took me by a lock of mine head; and the Spirit lifted me up between the earth and the heaven, and brought me in the visions of God to Jerusalem, to the door of the inner gate that looketh toward the north; where was the seat of the image of jealousy, which provoketh to jealousy. And, behold, the glory of the God of Israel was there."*

Ruwach – now instead of carrying him, it lifts him to the place of second heaven.

It is a glory above the glory of man upon the earth.

Outpouring into the streets- **Acts 2:5**

3. The Glory Moves To The Door Of The House

This is an <u>HONORING glory</u> of His character

Ezekiel 9:3 *"And the glory of the God of Israel was gone up from the cherub,* *whereupon he was, to the threshold of the house."*

This is a glory of entrance. A glory that requires sanctification.

Ezekiel 9:4 *"mark upon the foreheads of the men that sigh and that cry for all the abominations that be done in the midst thereof."*

Acts 3, Gate Beautiful

4. The Glory Fills The Court to the point of touching the Cherubim

This is His <u>FILLING GLORY</u> --- Requires HIS Presence

Ezekiel 10:4 *"Then the glory of the LORD went up from the cherub, and stood over the threshold of the house; and the house was filled with the cloud, and the court was full of the brightness of the LORD's glory."*

Ezekiel 10:18 (KJV 1900) — *18 Then the glory of the LORD departed from off the threshold of the house, and stood over the cherubim.*

Acts 4:31

5. The Glory Moves To The Eastern Gate

This is a **DIVIDING Glory** --- Requires holiness

Ezekiel 10:18-19 *"Then the glory of the LORD departed from off the threshold of the house, and stood over the cherubim… the wheels also were beside them, and every one stood at the door of the east gate of the LORD's house; and the glory of the God of Israel was over them above."*

A national purging glory

Acts 5

6. The Glory Moves To The Mountain On The East

A COVENANTAL ALIGNMENT GLORY --- ONENESS – FORMED CORPORATE MAN

Ezekiel 11:1 (KJV 1900) — *1 Moreover the spirit lifted me up, and brought me unto the east gate of the LORD's house, which looketh eastward: and behold at the door of the gate five and twenty men; among whom I saw Jaazaniah the son of Azur, and Pelatiah the son of Benaiah, princes of the people.*

The Spirit --- the breath --- ruwach of God lifts him again
The third breath

These 25 men were the *Ecclesia* or government of the city

Acts 6, first half

7. The Glory Fills the House he has built and He is now in the House!

This is <u>TRANSPARENT glory</u> or transcended glory

Ezekiel 43:5–7 (KJV 1900) — 5 *So the Spirit took me up, and brought me into the inner court; and, behold, the glory of the LORD filled the house. 6 And I heard him speaking unto me out of the house; and the man stood by me. 7 And he said unto me, Son of man, the place of my throne, and the place of the soles of my feet, where I will dwell in the midst of the children of Israel for ever, and my holy name, shall the house of Israel no more defile, neither they, nor their kings, by their whoredom, nor by the carcasses of their kings in their high*

places.

The fourth breath

The corporate man is formed and He is now dwelling in the house.

We become a doorway to heaven as they peer into us, they see heaven because of our transparency.

These will be outward coming from an inward work.

Chapter 7

The Glory and Breath in Acts

As we have seen these seven glories and four breaths in Ezekiel, is there a pattern we can recognize in scripture? The answer is: yes, the book of Acts holds all of these as well. Let's start with the first one.

The Glory With The Captivity. This is an ILLUMINATON Glory, Acts 1

The early Church had such promises but still lacked true illumination into the purposes of God. Even the seasoned disciples had returned to their old lifestyles after the Resurrection. There seemed to be a spiritual captivity sitting upon the Church. They had not yet had an encounter with the Holy Spirit and it appeared that all but a few had lost hope. But the breath brought them from the place of captivity to the upper room. They had been watchmen and now they were still being called out to be watchmen. There was a real need for relationships to be formed within all those who had experienced the encounters with

Jesus. They had all benefited but had not really entered into that life giving flow of God that comes from His nature residing within. They had only known it as a force coming towards them from without. The breath of God carried them to the place God's glory was resting, the upper room. They had to make a decision to be obedient. Without the encounter promised them, they would go back to the current religious structures that had no life.

Acts 2:1

The Glory At The Inner Gate Of The Temple, Acts 2, Freedom Glory

As they had gathered in obedience and basically, like Ezekiel, were silent for almost 40 days. The rest of the world was going on. Christ had come and departed and the desire to slip back to old traditions was beginning to overtake them. But instead of convincing everyone to hold fast, they had gathered to first hold fast themselves. They had been promised that they would be endued with power from on high. The word 'power' is the word *dunamis*. It is more than just the explosive power of God that actually means *'the very nature of God residing within a person*'. Without this nature first deposited within them, everything that they would do would not be able to carry or project a breath of God. As we know, the outpouring came with great power. It was more than just speaking in tongues, but the grace of Isaiah, the Spirit of understanding, had come upon them as well. They doubted the purposes of God towards all men. It was a FREEDOM glory that they were experiencing. It brought deliverance, expressiveness, and outward portrayal of the nature of God that was residing within them. They were now in a place above the Glory of man upon the earth and resting in second heaven. They had been given a place of stewarding the great mysteries of God.

As the outpouring swept from the upper room upon the streets, others were able to experience not just speaking in tongues and the movement of the Spirit, but they were being encountered by the very nature of God. The nature of God is what brings the true freedom in God. The Holy Spirit's activity in our life removes the obstacles for us to experience that freedom. The Holy Spirit is not necessarily the freedom, but the nature of

God residing with us and has no limitation or boundaries restraining it. Unlike the Holy Spirit's activity, which is restrained by the yieldedness of man participating, once the nature of God is present within an individual, true liberty begins to unfold. Where the Spirit of the Lord is, there is liberty!

The Glory Moves To The Threshold Of The House, Acts 3, Gate Beautiful

Like Ezekiel, the glory was resting at the entrance point to the temple. The glory had moved from the upper room to the street and now to the entrance point of the temple and a man's heart. Remember, this is a glory of entrance. A glory that requires sanctification. By healing the man at the Gate Beautiful, God was also freeing him from all ridicule of something wrong with him that caused him to be in this condition. This is an honoring glory that reveals the character of Christ. The healing of the man also revealed the nature of God within Peter and John. You cannot give something away unless you first possess it. They didn't bring healing but had the nature of healing within them. The display showed there was no physical limitation for God touching people. God not only honored the man at the gate but also honored Peter and John for faithfully going to pray and to be willing to be used. As they stepped out, God stepped in.

The required sanctification had come for this man. No longer could he be denied from the temple as unclean because of his physical condition. He was freed from all limitations and the first thing he did after receiving strength was to go into the temple. He was allowed entrance! The crowd gathered on Solomon's porch, the threshold of entrance, the **133rd Psalm** of the fifteen Psalms they recited as they entered the temple, before going in. Peter then preached to those gathered at the threshold of the temple. But it is more than the threshold of a temple, but a threshold of entrance into knowing the King and entering His Kingdom.

The Glory Fills The Court to the point of touching the Cherubim

Now with the glory in motion, the Church moves deeper into God. In **Acts 4:31**, Peter is "filled" with the Holy Spirit when he speaks. They were so full of God and His nature that no man was willing to come against them. They commanded them not to speak in His name but their response was that they could not be quiet. In verse 24, with *one accord*, which means '*a passion that is boiling and running together*', that they made a request of God to be able to speak with even more boldness. God had indeed honored them and His character was resting upon them. When they had prayed, the place was shaken and in verse 31, it says they were all filled with the Holy Ghost and spoke the Word of God with boldness. This boldness was coming forth from the nature of God within them. They simply requested that that portion of the nature of God be loosed. The outcome was the multitude of them who believed was of one heart and one soul. They had all things common. There was great power and great grace upon them all. Signs, wonders, and miracles were loosed. People were selling lands and houses and laying them at the apostles' feet. This was not done to restructure the social status. Since they had all things common, which was the Kingdom of God to advance, the provision was to remove any physical limitation of fulfilling this mandate. This is a filling Glory and it requires His presence. His presence had literally invaded the early Church and was empowering them to be set apart.

The Glory Moves To The Eastern Gate a DIVIDING Glory --- Requires holiness- Acts 5

Just as God desires us to enter in, we must also enter in the proper way. In **Acts 5**, Ananias and Sapphira desired to be a part but their heart was divided. They did not really believe God could take care of them. But God was building more than a small group of people meeting because they believed or experienced the same thing. God was building a spiritual nation. A nation filled with power, wonderment and His nature.

Just like Ezekiel saw the glory standing over the mercy seat in **Ezekiel 10**, the provision for mercy and grace was always present. It was whether we would take advantage of it. Obviously Ananias and Sapphira had plotted their actions out and had come into agreement. What they were actually doing was lying not to Peter but to God. They were coming against the now present and tangible grace of God resting upon His people. The decision to withhold some of the profits yet say their whole heart was engaged would not be tolerated.

This only example of severe judgment in the New Testament tells me there was a much deeper offense than what is written. Being people of wealth would mean they were also people of extreme influence. God would use this situation to bring reverential fear to a spiritual nation.
The speculation can go on and on for the reasoning of why but the reality is, it did happen! This Glory is a purging glory and requires more than sanctification but holiness. Holiness is the setting apart unto God. I believe their actions were not only coming upon the grace resting upon the emerging Church but also coming against the holiness the Church was walking in. It is obvious to look at things in a holistic way and we soon see this. In **Acts 4**, they had all things common, grace was upon them and needs were being met. In **Acts 6**, the needs are not

being met and the commonality talked about up to this point, has diminished. In between, is **Acts 5** and this story. God was purging a nation.

But the nature of God could not be stopped. Sick are healed by the very shadow of Peter. Scientists say that we put out a brain wave that is measurable about 6 inches around our head. They now have discovered a measurable "brain type" wave that comes from our heart. It is measurable about 8 feet around us. Peter's shadow was the nature of God radiating from his spirit man. The people healed by his shadow simply got in the "zone" and the presence of God radiating from him, healed them!

The Glory Moves To The Mountain On The East
A COVENANTAL ALIGNMENT GLORY --- ONENESS – FORMED CORPORATE MAN - Acts 6

Now we come to **Acts 6** and the multiplication that had occurred in spite of Ananias and

Sapphira was requiring more from everyone. The Church begins to take charge of setting in place the due order and legislating from a spiritual advantage point. First order is the order of "Common". This was the removal of the hindrances from the apostles to be able to spend time in prayer and study. The appointment of Stephen and the seven men *full of the Holy Spirit* is the first governmental pact the Church did. Because of setting these things in order, the Word of God increased and the disciples were multiplied. Scripture says that even a great number of the priests believed. A study of history shows that the numbers are believed to be 8,000 priests that made the conversion! The simple starting and setting in place governmentally of the seven men released a paradigm shift in the governing body of the spiritual nation. There was about to be an overthrow of who was truly governing things in the spiritual realm. This new breath of God that had blown into the Church was a governing breath to begin to govern the city and set in place the *Ecclessia* as a force to be reckoned with within the culture.

The Glory Fills the House He has built and He is now in the House!

This is TRANSPARENT glory or transcended glory.

Ezekiel 43:5–7 (KJV 1900) — 5 *So the spirit took me up, and brought me into the inner court; and, behold, the glory of the L*ORD *filled the house. 6 And I heard him speaking unto me out of the house; and the man stood by me. 7 And he said unto me, Son of man, the place of my throne, and the place of the soles of my feet, where I will dwell in the midst of the children of Israel for ever, and my holy name, shall the house of Israel no more defile, neither they, nor their kings, by their whoredom, nor by the carcases of their kings in their high places.*

The fourth breath now comes and the corporate man is formed and dwelling in the house. We barely begin to see this in the rest of the book of Acts as the Church and the voices and disciples of the Church become living doorways to heaven. No matter where they go, the presence of God is with them and the Holy Spirit is leading them. Their lives are transparent and when people see them, they see the Christ through them. The people seemed to be amazed and they probably tried to look for the 'old man' they once knew but could no longer find them. The corporate man has been formed in the presence of God dwelling in this house that has been built. People are coming to peer as if into heaven itself as they peer into these lives. The expansion of the Church alters humanity, the earth, and all creation. All men are feeling its effects and all men fear God once again. As the disciples of the apostles traveled to the known earth, the whole earth is coming into the knowledge of the Glory of the Lord as the waters cover the sea.

The disciples easily embraced martyrdom. What they were offering spread like wildfire. They were not just offering some gifts of the Spirit or some promises from God but the very nature of God to be formed inside of people. People were taking on the image of Christ to the point that at Antioch, they called them 'Christ like' for the very first time. The birthing of the nature of Jesus upon the earth would forever change the earth and all people living on it. The disciples were beginning to see just how far reaching it was becoming. His death and resurrection power would touch and change the course of all things. Their faith was ignited to fulfill the Kingdom purpose and intention of God for the moment that they lived in.

This is why they suffered so many things, embraced so many things, and sacrificed their lives unto death. Their perspective was eternal and not temporal. Their perspective was Kingdom and not selfish. Their perspective was coming from the nature of God and not from a promise given them. They were seeing through His eyes, feeling His heart and hearing His voice. That is why Paul could say such things ***as greater is He that is in us than he that is in the world*** and ***we are a new creature in Christ Jesus and old things have passed away***. Their understanding of the promises of God and what the Holy Spirit was saying was of a far greater understanding than today. We must realize that what we read and embrace as New Testament scripture, they were living it before they wrote it down. Today we read about it in hopes that we can move in that. There's a great void between the two and the only thing that can fill the void is the nature of God and the breath of God being released from that nature.

His Nature Formed - His Breath Released

Chapter 8

The Breath of God

Genesis 2:7 (KJV 1900) — 7 *And the Lord God formed man of the dust of the ground, and breathed into his nostrils the breath of life; and man became a living soul.*

The first place we see the breath of God is when God spoke the universe into existence. His voice of authority coming from His creative nature placed everything into existence as we see it. But when He made man from that creation, He breathed into him. Man was set aside as different from the rest of creation. The hand of God formed him from creation. In some ways, man represents that creation because his form has substance from creation. Man could be said to be the sum total of all creation!

God did more than just speak man into existence; His very hands touched and formed him. Imagine God could have spoken man into existence like the rest of creation when God said "let us make man in our image." Now with that thought, we also see that all creation was a representation of God as well. The image formed was taken from what God had created with His authority. His authority actually was resting in His creation.

God took the very dust of the earth, the minerals and deposits and brought them together in such a way with His "Hands" that the human form was created. That's why God can create miracles, restore what was lost and has said the works of our hands are blessed. We are actually the blessing of His hands!

But man stood different than all other creation, so different that the form of life needed was beyond the creative authority to be set in place. No, God would do something more unique, He would breathe into Him. When He breathed into him, he placed His very nature inside Adam and he became a "living being". Creation received the life flow of God but man received the life nature of God as well.

The word 'breath' means '*inspiration, the Spirit, breath from God*'. Man did not just receive life like the rest of creation, he received breath. He received the inspiration of God. Inspiration comes from God's nature. God gave man the creative nature that inspires.

That's why we create inventions, inquire into science, draw artwork, write poetry, play instruments that we have invented, etc. It is not just coming because of how we are wired but because of the Divine nature inside of us.

This breath did more than make us stand to our feet or come alive from the dead. It actually was a life-giving breath that brought the ability to sustain this life. The word 'life' means '*living, reviving, relative, to be quickened, to be sustained, to be alive, to have life, to remain life, to sustain life*'. This breath of life or nature of sustaining, formed man into a living being, a living soul, a spiritual being with capacity for serving and fellowshipping with God.

Genesis 7:15 (KJV 1900) — 15 And they went in unto Noah into the ark, two and two of all flesh, wherein is the breath of life.

It is interesting that when Noah was saving the animals and had built the ark, they were drawn not to the ark for the saving of their lives, but they were drawn to the "Breath of Life". Noah is the only other person in the Bible besides Enoch that pleased God and there is a reference to what he was carrying.

The story is written that he and his sons and wife went first into the ark then the animals came. It says in **Genesis 7:15** that "they went in unto". It does not say they were herded in or led in with halters, etc. But the animals on their own accord, came. This was a drawing to the nature of God in Noah. The drawing to the Breath of Life.

You see whatever 'ark' we are laboring and building for the future in which the Lord has commanded us, still is empty until His breath is within it. But once within, it saves not just us but our whole family. Even though Noah's family was not entirely right with God, the breath Noah carried brought them to salvation. Once the breath is inside our containers of ministry, it will draw others. If animals can be drawn, surely humanity will be drawn.

So when did this breath become reality? In *Genesis 7:1,* it says God saw in Noah righteousness in his generation. Imagine that! One man's righteousness could save his family and the entire world. This shouldn't be a surprise as that's exactly what Jesus did at the cross.

The Breath of God

Genesis 6:4–8 (KJV 1900) — *4 There were giants in the earth in those days; and also after that, when the sons of God came in unto the daughters of men, and they bare children to them, the same became mighty men which were of old, men of renown. 5 And GOD saw that the wickedness of man was great in the earth, and that every imagination of the thoughts of his heart was only evil continually. 6 And it repented the LORD that he had made man on the earth, and it grieved him at his heart. 7 And the LORD said, I will destroy man whom I have created from the face of the earth; both man, and beast, and the creeping thing, and the fowls of the air; for it repenteth me that I have made them. 8 But Noah found grace in the eyes of the LORD.*

There was evil unlike anything we have seen today. Fallen angels (the sons of God) were mating with the women of the earth and an offspring of giants had been birthed. (See the book of Jubilees, can be found online, for more insight into this) These children had become leaders of the evil. The evil was so bad that the thoughts of men were continuously evil. The word 'imagination' means *'form, plan, device and purpose'*. Every day as man awoke; he set out an intentional plan and purpose that what would be accomplished that day focused only on evil.

The Lord saw the evil that had come upon the earth. He was so upset He even wanted to destroy what had been created. But Noah became the answer to God's rage with His creation. He found grace in the sight of God!

The word 'grace' used here means *'favor, acceptance, favorable'*. It comes from a root word meaning *'to make or create favor, or acceptance, or to make gracious to the point that favor can be directed to'*.

You see, God always has a plan of redemption even when it seems as if there is no real way. Noah had been kept by God in the midst of evil. He had allowed the original nature of God in Adam to be formed in himself. It had made him righteous to the point he would save God's creation. It brought him to the point of obedience in doing what others mocked and ridiculed. He built an ark on dry land when it had never rained before. For years he labored and God was forming righteousness s and nature inside of him for something yet to come. It formed something so deep in him that he eventually carried God's creative breath. A breath that would change history and set the course.

As I was studying some things out for the writing of this book, I found something very interesting that we have overlooked. It is what I would call a key to effectiveness. After Jesus was resurrected, he gave three commissionings. For the most part, we only look at two and most of the time combine them as one and miss seeing the uniqueness of them. Let's look at all three and see the pattern we have missed.

Mark 16:15–18 (KJV 1900) — *15 And he said unto them, Go ye into all the world, and preach the gospel to every creature. 16 He that believeth and is baptized shall be saved; but he that believeth not shall be damned. 17 And these signs shall follow them that believe; In my name shall they cast out devils; they shall speak with new tongues; 18 They shall take up serpents; and if they drink any deadly thing, it shall not hurt them; they shall lay hands on the sick, and they shall recover.*

The disciples had moved to Galilee just outside

of Jerusalem. This story is unfolding shortly after the resurrection. In **Mark 16:7**, it says Peter went to Galilee. In verse **14**, Jesus appeared to the disciples and upbraided them for their unbelief and hardness of heart. The word 'upbraided' means '*deserved reproach*', and it comes from a root word meaning '*shame*'. What had they done to receive such harsh treatment? After all, the resurrection had just occurred and they were still sorting things out. But Jesus said it was because of not believing the report of the two along the way. Is it about them believing the report of the risen Christ or is it really about the fact that others could experience the risen Christ? Perhaps the answer lies in a commissioning we have overlooked.

Jesus commissioned us to make disciples in **Mark 16**. As we read this, we see it is about spiritual awakening. Awakening deals with the individual coming into understanding of Christ. What He was addressing with them would also indicate that others would be able to experience the risen Christ as well. Just like the two on the road who did believe, they too, would now be qualified for this commissioning of making disciples. This commissioning has a key word in it we all like to focus on, "Go". Just like the other commissioning we are familiar with in **Matthew 28**.

Matthew 28:18–20 (KJV 1900) — *18 And Jesus came and spake unto them, saying, All power is given unto me in heaven and in earth. 19 Go ye therefore, and teach all nations, baptizing them in the name of the Father, and of the Son, and of the Holy Ghost: 20 Teaching them to observe all things whatsoever I have commanded you: and, lo, I am with you alway, even unto the end of the world. Amen.*

The word 'go' is a verb. It requires action. It means '*to depart, to lead over, carry over, and transfer. To pursue the journey on which one has entered, or to continue on one's journey*'. The definition points to one thing mainly and that is something has already been in motion, more so than something about to go into motion. It comes from a root word meaning '*a trial, experience, attempt. To attempt a thing, to make trial of a thing or of a person. To have a trial of a thing. To experience, learn to know by experience*'. So it really is focused upon not so much the knowing before doing but the knowing coming after the doing.

Now remember the first commissioning we read occurred in Galilee, now this one is recorded as being on a mountain in Galilee, **Matthew 28: 16**. Some scholars believe it is the Mount of Olives as the disciples were retracing the steps of Jesus and remembering the Sermon on the Mount. It is obvious the locations are close to each other but distinctly different and so is the commissioning. The **Mark 16** commissioning is dealing with individuals but this one is now dealing with nations. This is truly reformation to shift or align entire nations into order with Kingdom principles. Reformation always deals with groups of people. This commissioning has the word 'go' in it as well.

It seems we have always been real good in the 'going' or at least pushing 'the going'. The reality is that most people are reluctant to go. I have always wondered, "Why is this so hard to motivate people in doing the work of ministry?" After all, we have "orders" to go!

But the question is maybe more than an obedience question but one that asks "how will this be done"? Our conclusion is generally by the power of the Holy Spirit found in ***Acts 2 or 1 Cor. 12***. But Jesus commissioned us to be sent with His nature in ***John 20***. You see the commission we have overlooked is the "how to be sent" the other two commissions are what we are to accomplish when we "Go". Our reluctance to go is entirely related to not knowing we have been sent!

So what is this third commissioning we have so seriously overlooked? The first two we saw concerned what we would do. But Jesus actually commissioned us to be "sent" first with 'the how'.

John 20:19–23 (KJV 1900) — *19 Then the same day at evening, being the first day of the week, when the doors were shut where the disciples were assembled for fear of the Jews, came Jesus and stood in the midst, and saith unto them, Peace be unto you. 20 And when he had so said, he shewed unto them his hands and his side. Then were the disciples glad, when they saw the Lord. 21 Then said Jesus to them again, Peace be unto you: as my Father hath sent me, even so send I you. 22 And when he had said this, <u>he breathed on them</u>, and saith unto them, Receive ye the Holy Ghost: 23 Whose soever*

sins ye remit, they are remitted unto them; and whose soever sins ye retain, they are retained.

This commissioning is the closest one to the resurrection. They were in fear for their lives. In **John 20:19**, it says the first day of the week and it is evening time on the same day, which is resurrection day. The disciples had shut the doors and settled in some form of a room or home. They were not on a mountain, they were not traveling to Galilee and they were still in Jerusalem.

Jesus appeared and spoke to their fears confronting their unbelief as well. He then began with the first words being their commissioning. This is just like God to get 'down to business'. This commission is the actual sending forth. The word 'sent' is the same word for apostle, *apostellos*. He is saying "I am your apostle and I am sending you in the same authority and way as apostles. In the same manner as I have been sent, so send I you". He was sent as a son. He was sent as a representative of God. He was sent as a healer, deliverer, etc. He was sent as truth. We can make an endless list, but the reality is He was sent as the nature of God. He was sending His disciples out the same way, as the nature of God on display for all to see.

He breathed His nature on them. It is the resurrected breath coming from the resurrected nature of God. The word 'breath' is not about blowing in and out but a single direction of blowing and imparting from what is within. He then says 'receive the Holy Spirit'. Many believe that in this moment, they received the Holy Spirit, but the scriptures teach us that He told them to wait until they are endued with the Holy Spirit's power. We see they did not just "go" but did indeed wait. They had the nature, now they needed the empowerment of that nature and then the disciples would go and the nations would turn.

We have it so backward. We want the Holy Spirit to form the nature within us, when in reality we need God to breathe His nature on us. We want the manifestations of God without the nature of God connected to them. The nature of God will require the death of self at our cross. It truly will require the laying down of self and all self serving ideology. It will require for us to be resurrected by that nature and rise up to be the exceeding great army of Ezekeil. They knew the nature of God

--- Jesus standing before them. But they did not know the Holy Spirit yet.

Jesus did say "***receive ye the Holy Ghost***". The word 'receive' means '*to take and make your own*'. But when we look at the words 'Holy Spirit' in the text, it refers in the Greek, to the Holy Spirit as a name not a presence! You see the original language shows they had to take hold of the Holy Spirit at a later time. I wonder if this is why we have so much trouble getting people to move with the Holy Spirit. Are we trying to attach the Holy Spirit to our unholy nature or to parts still not fully redeemed? It seems to me the effectiveness of Christ upon the earth was because of the Holy Spirit's activity working through a vessel with the nature of God.

Then Jesus says something to them in **verse 23 *Whose soever sins ye remit, they are remitted unto them; and whose soever sins ye retain, they are retained***.

The word 'remit' means '*to send away or depart, to expire, to let go*'. The word 'retain' means '*to have power, to take hold of, seize a person, to not let go*'. Basically He is saying "if you release them, then they are released and if you do not release them, they will be held". Now that is not coming from the gifts of the Spirit to release from sin but more so from the nature releasing them.

These 3 commissionings were not new but an extension of Jesus' own commissioning. He did all three and expects no less from us. He was passing the baton to His disciples who have passed it throughout the ages to us today. So the question is HOW ARE WE STEWARDING THESE COMMISSIONINGS?

Jesus went down somewhat the same pathway as Noah. He became righteousness thus releasing the nature of God upon the earth to be formed in Him. His 'ark' was called the Cross for the saving of the world. The breath of life draws us to that Cross. After resurrection, Jesus came to His disciples and put in motion a plan to save the world. They would become the new 'ark'.

In **John 20**, Jesus came to the disciples shortly after being resurrected. He died and now had risen. Without the death process in our lives as well, we will never have the nature of God resident in force within us. Without death, there is still the fleshly sin nature trying to gain access. It does not take death alone but also resurrection. Jesus was raised in "Power" the nature of God raised Him! Many experience a raising of themselves but it is more intellectual ascent than a real death process that requires new life to flow.

Today we hear very little preaching of the Cross. Very little on dying to self and taking up our own cross. Perhaps we have lost track of the important element that John the Baptist said. "I must decrease so He can increase". It is not us waiting for Him to increase and crowd out our old nature. It is us making room for His nature to fill even more and more of the corners of our heart.

The words had not fully convinced them but when He breathed on them, something changed! I believe Jesus was restoring the nature to man just like at the first, with Adam. He then went to the Cross to free man from sin, completing the pattern of redemption intentioned since the fall. They had an encounter with the resurrected Christ. The very nature of God in purest form was standing before them. Jesus calmed their fears and then He breathed on them without warning or explanation. Jesus was called the

The Breath of God

last Adam and He transferred that nature to His disciples when He breathed on them. Remember the breath of life is to sustain life. Just like Noah had sustained life so now the disciples had the ability to sustain spiritual life because of the nature given in this moment. Jesus was sending them not just with anointing but with His breath, His very nature. Today we send with anointing but Jesus sent with His nature.

When Jesus breathed on them, they did not receive the Holy Spirit in that moment. What He was referring to was their next assignment after they received the nature of God, and that was to receive the empowerment of the Holy Spirit that was coming. He told them to wait until they were endued from on high. The word 'endued' means '*to be wrapped in or enveloped in*'. God wanted His nature both protected outwardly and connected internally to His nature. For the most part today, we are very backward. We want the power but don't have the nature.

The Holy Spirit at Pentecost in **Acts 2** gave the ability to demonstrate this life by empowering the lack in man that had not yet let the nature fully form. In our weakness, He is strong. The greatest area of weakness is our flesh and the nature of God is the greatest way of making us strong. This nature with the anointing of God empowering the weakness of flesh, now that was the display that caused people to cry out to be saved. That's what caused 5000 to be born again in a moment. That's what the early Church had that everyone desired to peer into and to be a part. The nature and the Spirit, the essence of God and the empowerment of our lack. That is attractive!

We see the wind blowing in **Acts 2** and believe it is the breath of God. That wind was not the nature of God coming but the Holy Spirit coming to carry man to the next assignment in the Spirit. It was bringing the sounds from heaven into that place as they heard the heavenly language being uttered. It was carrying the fire of holiness from heaven as well and each man saw the power of heaven that could rest on an individual. The wind was fueling the fire and gave utterance to the nature residing inside those who had gathered. You can only imagine the disciples telling them of waiting and also telling of this breath that Jesus breathed on them. You see each one of us has to contend for the nature and breath of God. They tarried for 40+ days in the Upper

Room. Many of us today are not willing to even tarry an hour. We want everything imparted or handed to us without suffering for it or wrestling to attain. This has caused us to devalue almost everything God has given to us.

The wind, the unseen force, goes where it wills. The Holy Spirit carries us much the same way as He wills. The wind blows and brings rains and change of seasons. So does the Holy Spirit. The Holy Spirit at Pentecost became the guide for the nature and breath of God. The Holy Spirit became the one alongside that could testify and bring witness of the very nature. The Holy Spirit would manifest through God's sons and daughters and would confirm the nature with the signs and wonders of the Spirit.

You see, Jesus said in **John 14:16**: "***I will pray the Father, and he shall give you another Comforter, that he may abide with you forever***" It was not in the plan of God for us to have the Holy Spirit until Jesus made the request to the Father. Jesus had seen how the Holy Spirit affected His body in the flesh and knew humanity would benefit from it. So this divine anointing has come upon us to do one thing, be witnesses. To supernaturally do what we in our own selves could not do.

Back to **John 20**, Jesus was telling them that He was sending them out as the nature of God upon the earth; they would be empowered by the Holy Spirit, be led by Him, fed by Him, comforted by Him, etc., and then free people from sin!

So this is the assignment, now here is what is needed to unfold it. Let me breathe this nature into you with my breath. The word 'breath' here means '*the act of blowing outward*'. It comes from a root word meaning '*a twofold hope*'. He was saying 'let me give the nature of my two fold hope into you!

Now what is that two fold hope? you might ask. First, the hope of eternal life, everlasting life, freedom from sin. Eternity in all its glory. This is our hope coming from resurrection. The second hope is to live <u>now</u> above these things, to live Kingdom life now. To live in victory now. To work for God and do the things Jesus did. Jesus was that hope for the people walking upon the earth. The two fold hope was <u>be</u> the nature like Jesus and to minister like Him from the nature of God while being empowered by the Holy Spirit and

The Breath of God

allowing that nature, like Enoch, to take you into the eternal realm!

It was the breath of life --- the same breath that was blown into Adam to cause him to be the first born. It was the same breath that raised the first Adam and now was going to raise Jesus from the dead. This breath would raise a people from deadness to be ones called out for Him with His nature dwelling within. Now the breath comes to bring forth the last born Adam on the earth through the *Ecclesia*. It is a breath that raises us into the supernatural life.

You see, we minister mainly today from anointing and not from the nature of God. But the nature of God will speak to people and they will be free from sin in a moment. The nature of God is not waiting for the right moment but creates the moment to release God's intentions. The nature of God is not transferable but is something each person must decide to pursue and receive. The disciples were not following Jesus for three years because He was the son of God and they knew it. They thought it but were not convinced of it and it showed when He died how they all lost hope. No, they were drawn to the nature of God walking the earth. Today we are drawn to people's personalities and anointing connected with them. We need to draw people to the nature of God and allow that nature and not a personality or anointing to confront them.

The nature of God sets a standard that requires no words of explaining or convincing. It makes people see truth in ways never before sought after and creates environments for the Holy Spirit's activity to be fulfilled. It convicts by God's presence. It confronts by God's presence. It shifts by God's presence. It awakens the heart by God's presence. I think you see the difference.

Another place in scripture where we can see the breath of God spoken of is **Ezekiel 37** with the vision of the dry bones. The story takes on the same outline of creation. A coming together, a fitting by what would be spoken. Just like Adam was spoken out of a thought of taking on the image of God, so in this story it is a single corporate man being formed. A warring army seen as not many people fighting in a battle but rather a singular army.

Ezekiel 37:5 (KJV 1900) — *5 Thus saith the*

The Breath of God

Lord GOD unto these bones; Behold, I will cause breath to enter into you, and ye shall live:

Again God says He will breathe on them and they will be resurrected. They will experience life. It will take the breath of God to raise an army in the hour we are living. The breath will come once we come together. The coming together is not unity, nor agreement, nor participating in each other's gatherings. The common thread here is the same one of **John 17**, to be united in common purpose because of Christ. When we finally decide to work for the same purpose or see each person working for the same purpose, and we are truly hidden in Christ, then the breath will come.

You see, it requires us to truly be led by the Spirit like Ezekiel was. In verse 1, he said he was led by the Spirit and brought into the midst of these dry bones. He described them as very many and very dry. Meaning it was beyond the typical that you would expect. By the same token, it will take something beyond the typical that we expect to bring the breath of God into so many who are lost and hope is cut off.

His Nature Formed - His Breath Released

It took someone who would not look at circumstances to speak to the bones, to prophesy to the bones and then to release the four winds of God to come and breathe into them. Those four winds are the four faces of God that Ezekiel saw in the first chapter and the four Gospels showing the four sides of Christ's nature.

This breath is a breath that connects us, not to enter into the eternal realm, but to <u>be</u> in the eternal realm. It was from that place that Ezekiel was to speak and prophesy. It was from that place that the four winds would come. It was from that place that the breath would bring life. The outcome: an exceeding great army would arise!

What would make this army great was it had conquered death! It was raised in power and great glory. It was carrying the nature and breath of God!

Chapter 9

The Breath As It Comes

I am looking for those people who are carrying the breath of God. All believers have had an encounter with the Son of God. Most believers have encounters with the Holy Spirit of God. We also have encounters with anointing, His presence, and other dynamics of the creative forces that come from the throne.

But the breath of God is something different. We see in scripture there are four winds that blow. We see Moses having an almost 'face to face' with God. We even see Jesus breathing on them and "they received the Holy Ghost". This breath is more than a onetime encounter but it sets a creative force of God in motion in our lives. It is more than an anointing or a gift of the Spirit to meet a need. It is the release of the intentions of God's creative voice for the moment of time to come into a moment to forever shift a person.

As those called to be the *Ecclesia* and govern the earth, we are also called to be the Melchizedek priesthood upon the earth. That means we have access into heaven and implement the throne into people's hearts. This cannot come with words of man's wisdom but has to be as the Spirit (*pneuma* – the breath) of God is allowed to be released from us. The breath of God carries an anointing with it but it is the enablement, not for us to perform a certain gifting, but the anointing in this exists to be able to yield to allow the Spirit within to have full expression outward. The breath is about words from God's heart to our heart in the divine *kairos* moment. The breath comes not as an anointing <u>upon</u> us, but it actually releases an anointing from *within* us.

The breath of God comes from deep in our spirit. I can only tell you what I have experienced and perhaps that will help. At times I can sense the presence of God so close or the anointing seemingly present and just under the surface in my spirit. It is like a layer inside me has become alive to the purpose of God and it requires me to act or speak. But with the breath, it is not from that surface layer in my spirit but comes from the deepest part of me. It comes almost like turning my insides out so all can see. You see it has to pass through the surface anointing, that enablement of God. But it is not just that enablement being released but that which is deeper. So we can either minister from that close to the surface place of our spirit or from the place where deep (extreme) calls to deep (extreme).

The only way I can describe it is as if God is manifesting through me and I am completely yielded to Him moving out of me. When the breath of God comes and His release from my innermost being, the weight of it is almost overwhelming. When it happens to me occasionally when I'm preaching, there are times I teach the revelation God gives (anointing) and then there are times I close my eyes and preach with such conviction and depth. I don't have the scriptures I am speaking of memorized. I don't open my eyes and follow along with notes or even the Word. It is like one continuous revelation being released over the hour or so I am in this posture. I can pace a room with eyes fully closed and not run into things as God speaks directly to people.

It's as if my entire body has been yielded to the working of God through me. At times, the anointing and the presence is so thick that if I do open my eyes, it's as if I am blind and I cannot see. I can tell them the presence of God is so close, not only do I sense him, that I begin to feel oil from heaven dropping onto the top of my head. Even though no one else can see it, I can feel and sense it. So let me give you some examples and hopefully this will give you understanding as well.

Example 1- "Breath and Prophecy"

I was in a conference in Ohio where I had been asked to speak to a group of leaders. There was roughly about one hundred five-fold ministry leaders gathered in this conference. We had had several speakers already and the worship was OK and not what I would call a high level dynamic. The Spirit of the Lord began to come upon me in a very unique way. A word was being deposited in me that was going to be released in the meeting. I sensed that I was at a fork in the road in the spiritual realm. There was a strong anointing to release the word, but also the anointing to hold the word for a few minutes longer. Being in the prophetic office before God called me to be an apostle, I knew the longer a person holds a prophetic word, the greater the impact it carries. I have held words for long periods of time and even several at once. The greatest thing any prophet can learn is not just to hear the word but to understand the timing of releasing it. I decided to hold the word longer and as I did, I could sense it settling deeper in my spirit. It was as if it was going into a place that had never been opened before. The worship went on for about 20 more minutes and there was a speaker scheduled for that afternoon service.

As the worship came to an end and the music was still playing, there were a couple people that got up and gave some prophecy. I knew that we had transitioned to the place where the word inside of me was to be released. As I generally do, I waited until everyone was finished and came to the microphone to release that which was inside me. You see, when I get a prophetic word inside, I only get a few of the words. and they are general, mostly an overview of the prophetic word. I never get the word in fullness or line upon line or in full sentences. I began to open my mouth to prophesy the word and I could sense it coming from a very deep place in my spirit. It was not the typical way I usually felt. It was as if I could now sense two places that words could be deposited. The first was closest to the surface and was coming from an anointing. The second was deep in my spirit and coming from His nature.

I began to release the prophetic word over the five-fold ministry leaders from this deep place. It was a word specifically for them and not a general word of prophecy. The intensity of it came with such strength that I was shaking very violently under the force of delivering it. At one point, I was thinking to myself *"I don't even know if I'll be able to hang on to the microphone and may throw it out of my hands."*

I delivered the word which went on for almost 20 minutes under this kind of intensity. When I opened my eyes, (I never prophesy with my eyes opened as I won't be moved by what I see only what I hear), there was not a single person standing in the place. The power of the word as it came out of the nature of God with His breath, pushing it forth into the spirits of those gathered, had caused them to be unable to stand under the weight of the Glory that was released by it. My wife, Julie, was there

The Breath of God

with me and she was sitting in the back row. (We like to sit at the back when we visit other places so God can talk to us about His intentions for those gathered.) She said that the force of it had 'slain' people as it was being released. Many had tried to stand and were hanging onto their chairs until they could no longer hold on. Even the worship team was completely laid out on the platform and I was the only one left standing. I put the microphone back into the mic stand and sat down on a front chair.

After about 30 minutes, the pastor leading the conference got up from the floor and came to the mic and simply said, "There's nothing else to say, this meeting is finished, we will see you for tonight's meeting". He then fell back to the floor. As I looked around, the people remained in this posture before the Lord for over an hour. Slowly they got up but it was as if we had entered such a holy place that no one talked and everyone simply slipped away to get ready for the evening meeting.

Anointing in a prophetic word touches the soul and spirit of the person. It touches the intellect. The breath touches the origin point of their spirit, the deepest place. The breath comes to touch every molecule of our being and so it must also flow out of every molecule as well. This is the place from which all things flow.

Example 2 "Breath and Intercession"

I had been asked to conduct a prayer conference in Cleveland, Ohio. A good number of African intercessors were in attendance and the focus was to pray for our nation. I taught on the six types of prayer and the prayer of imprecation. We had intercession after each teaching session and then an evening meeting as well. It was a two day conference. At the Saturday morning session of the conference, the attendance was not very high when we opened, and my host seemed a little distraught by it. I told him not to worry and God would have His way with us.

By the time I got up to speak after the worship, the place had filled up. I taught on prayer again and can't recall what the topic was. We then began to go into intercession. The presence of God flooded my soul again and I went to the mic to speak over the people and

The Breath of God

help direct the intercession as it was unfolding. When I did, the seriousness of God came upon me and I began to decree over the people and the nation. The breath of God became so thick you could almost see it in the room. It was as if you had to yield to this breath in intercession or be pushed aside by it. It was coming through the room.

Intercession gripped people in new depths. The entire company of people began to weep. Weeping turned into wailing and wailing became uncontrollable. We were gripped with the heart of God. Every person fell prostrate before God- wailing. The intercession went through lunch and into the afternoon and even into the next session. It was as if it could not be turned off. Finally it settled down and we knew we had touched heaven. My host, a Nigerian, said he had never seen anything like it, not even in Nigeria. I agreed as I have made many trips to Nigeria and one thing about them, they know how to intercede and pray. Their prayer dynamic shames the American models. But this was so far beyond what we both had seen. Later he told me it forever changed the people who had gathered and a year later they were still talking about it.

The breath of God is so full of the life giving flow that it is as if it has no choice but to bring change, or create these types of moments. My simple obedience began to release the nature of prayer over a people.

Example 3 "Breath and Curses"

I was in Nigeria doing a leadership conference. Leaders had gathered in Akure and they had waited a long time for my coming. You see a prophetic dream was given that white men would come from the USA and would release revelation that would change the course of life as they knew it. They had waited over ten years for this promise to be fulfilled and here I was standing before them as part of the fulfillment.

I had brought teaching on the fivefold gifting and specifically the apostolic movement. Through the series of trips we conducted there over time, we planted almost 30 apostolic training schools graduating close to 6,000 students yearly. The way 'church' was done was changed because the message that I spoke had the breath or life giving flow and it shifted the region.

The Breath of God

But the story is a story within the story. There was an intersection within the city that the local witches had put a curse upon. The curse required a person each week to be killed by an automobile accident. And for 10 years, that is what happened each week. The pastors asked me what to do about it. I simply said "break the curse!" They asked me to do it I said "yes!" We literally left the meeting and walked about a 1/4mile away to the intersection. It was amazing how close we were to the actual location. When we got there, I had all the pastors get into a circle in the intersection. Three hundred fifty pastors held hands and made this huge circle while I stood in the midst of it.

Since this was one of the main intersections of the area, about 400,000 people pass through it, it began to back cars up in all directions as far as you could see over the hills, maybe 2 miles. At first, people were honking their horns in impatience. But they soon recognized it was the pastors of the city that were gathered. They got out of their cars and knelt down along the side of the road. It was an unbelievable sight to see. It was also refreshing to see the respect they had for the pastors of their city! The presence of the Lord began to consume me and I boldly stepped forth into the center of the circle and declared the curses at that intersection and all witchcraft over the city would be broken in Jesus' Name. I decreed for probably about five minutes then we broke the circle and began to be dismissed. Horns began honking and people began yelling and you could hear the roar of both cars and voices down all the streets and roads that had been blocked. There was great rejoicing in the people for what we had done because everyone knew the story of this intersection. The entire region of probably a million people soon heard what happened. From that day forward, there has not even been one accident in that intersection. The faith of the people was so large because of that day that it set in motion a chain of events over the next few years. It would cause this area that was in poverty to actually advance and become an area in Nigeria to grow economically in such a fashion that it was almost unrecognizable!

The breath of God does not just touch individuals but is so far reaching that it comes to shift nations and show forth the final authority of God that He is both King and Lord.

Example 4 "Breath and Restoration"

Our ministry was holding a small conference with a couple visiting speakers. The anticipation was running very high, and people had been pressing to have an encounter with God. As worship began for the evening service, the Lord spoke to me and said "you will not be delivering a message tonight. Your message will only have two words that will have My breath in it". As we were coming to the end of worship and while the music was still playing, I stepped forward to the microphone. Our team has been trained to hold a prophetic tension and worship until the next release of what God wants to do by His spirit, comes. That was exactly what they did and held the tension in the music. I simply said in short order that I had no message for the people tonight but I had two words that God had given me to speak over them and He would do the rest. I said "tonight, what God wants to do is this, "restore innocence!" The words went forth with the breath of God into the atmosphere and across the room. The weight of it was tangible and the outcome was almost unexpected. After probably one to two minutes, I still stood there with nothing else to say. I was not to explain what these words meant nor try to preach a message from this. You see, we get too impatient to allow the Holy Spirit to work so we try to step in to do His job. We must do only what God is telling us and leave room to trust the Holy Spirit's activity. In this moment, you could sense the Holy Spirit swirling in the room waiting for hearts to open so He could light upon them. Suddenly people began to cry sitting in the front of the room. It wasn't everybody but it was almost half of them. The Spirit moved from the front to the middle to the back and by the time He was done, probably half of those present were in tears and the Holy Spirit was working in their hearts and restoring innocence. This went on for about an hour. We then simply asked for testimonies and many came forward to speak of the wonder of God's healing virtue found in two words with the breath of God in them. There was no prayer line, there was no convincing of words, it was simply the breath of God that enabled the Holy Spirit to work.

The Breath of God

Example 5 "Breath and Deliverance"

I had just returned from a trip to Nigeria where I ministered with one of my good friends, Dr. Sammy Musepa from Pretoria, South Africa. We had been ministering together in Nigeria and I had planned a conference upon my return- roughly ten days later. Dr. Sammy was coming to the U.S. to be a part of this conference along with a prophet friend from Pennsylvania and two other ministers from Virginia Beach.

It was the first major conference we had done in a new ministry building. People came from all over, including a Pennsylvania congregation and former students from Indiana and Ohio. We had roughly 300 people present. We had several fivefold ministry people gathered as well. I held a short meeting the opening day with the leaders that I had scheduled to speak. I was asked what the plan was for the opening night. I said without even thinking or realizing it, "we're going demon hunting tonight!" They asked "what does that mean?" I said "we'll all find out when we get there!"

His Nature Formed - His Breath Released

You must remember, I had just returned from the African trip and while there, I had done a tremendous amount of deliverance. There seemed to be an anointing upon my life to stir up demonic activity. What I didn't realize was that I was carrying the breath and presence of God in a deep way.

As we started the service that night, the expectation was extremely high. The worship was very dynamic, very creative and prophetic. About halfway through the worship, the Lord spoke to me and said "Now free the people!" I went to the microphone and exhorted for a couple minutes about what it meant to truly be free. I then became more focused and said "if there is demonic activity or a stronghold in your life, then you need to be free so come forward and receive prayer." A line of about 30 people formed across the front. I was standing off to the side when I made the invitation. The Lord told me that all the demons were at the other end of the line as far away from me as they could get. We started down the line, my prophet friend from Pennsylvania and I, praying for people and seeing God set them free. We had reached a certain place in the line and I knew the next person we would pray

The Breath of God

for was demon possessed. I looked over at my friend without saying anything, but he said to me, "I know, let's go!" That very next person we prayed for had the demon manifest in a dramatic way. The person levitated off the floor and their tongue went out of their mouth almost 10 inches. Their eyes were rolled back in their head. We cast the demon out of this person and several more in line. We then reached a woman in which the demon was very strong. We bodily carried her from the sanctuary to a room behind the worship team and proceeded do deliverance on her.

I had already put some of my Bible School students in place to help with the deliverance and used it as a training session for them. We knew that deliverance can be very messy at times so we had buckets and towels in the deliverance room as well.

We cast the demon out of her as her whole family gathered around her. God then came and filled her with joy. Her entire family received the joy of the Lord. It was overflowing to the point of drunkenness. We literally drug her out of the room and just dropped her on the floor in front of the worship team and her family. The joy of the Lord began to spread through those gathered as they worshipped. The people applauded and yelled because of seeing them set free.

I then simply went and stood in front of people and if there was a demon in them, it would suddenly begin to manifest. Since I did not want to have the deliverance be the focal point of worship, we bodily carried the next person to the deliverance room. Once again, after they were delivered and God had filled them with joy, we deposited them in front of the worship team and the congregation. Everyone applauded even more.

This entire process went on repeatedly for the next hour or so. At one point, when we opened up the door to go back into the sanctuary, there was a line of people waiting to be delivered. I have never seen anything like this, ever. They had seen the freedom that came each time a person came out of the deliverance room and the congregation cheering with joy to see them set free.

This is what the breath and presence of God does for those that carry it. It causes demons

The Breath of God

to manifest and quake. It causes freedom and liberty to be released. It causes the people of God to rejoice, it causes the heart of God to be glad!

So the question is, how do we get this breath? It comes by putting the revelation that God gives, which is fresh breathed, deep into our spirit and allowing it to have residence there. Allowing it to become alive in us. It comes by being able to move and stir the first layer in our spirit, moving in the gifts, etc., so this passageway for the breath to flow through will not be a stoppage point. It comes by us deciding to go deeper in God and not settling for a substandard Christian expression. There is a decision point I have found each time I know that I must release what is deeper. It is a seemingly scary moment of totally losing control and allowing God to control my every molecule of being, right before the breath is released. It is a point of facing my fears and totally trusting God. Even while in the midst of the breath, the wrestling is with my flesh and desire to come back into a place of control. It is about a total faith walk. It is like I have told people before, I have preached a message in this place, had a vision occurring, and had God speak to me about personal things, all at the same time. I know that sounds 'out there' but I have experienced this several times. All of this comes from the deep origin point being released. When we prophesy and move in the gifts, we have a partial faith release. When we move in the breath, there is full release. There are no limitations in God.

Let me say this: I have been talking about a full, deep release. A corporate breath. At times, we do release the breath and don't know it. It is the times we minister to people one-on-one and what we speak is a 'now' word that carries life. It is not a memorized answer but comes from a place where we may not even know what we are saying. It creates life, releases hope and sets into motion- answers for a person. They may not even realize they have just been breathed on by God! We may not realize we have released His breath as well.

Every day we breathe in and out about 25,000 times with our natural lungs. We don't think about it, we just do it. We don't use our faith for it; we are just in faith and trust that the next breath will be there. The same is true with the breath of God, it is to be a natural

The Breath of God

thing. As we practice breathing His breath, in everyday life, then when we enter a race for souls, or a corporate event, we become more aware of the breath. We can even reach a point of intentional awareness of how we breathe so we can finish strong. So what am I saying? We must practice the breath so it becomes natural to us.

His Nature Formed - His Breath Released

Chapter 10

Greater Works

What will it take for us to do greater works? Do we have some misconceptions about what this really means? After all, we have a lot of things already in place yet it seems we have not done the greater works. Perhaps it is unfolding or perhaps it is yet to come. Both of these are true.

The words "greater work" is only listed two times in the New Testament. The works of God are referred to only a few more times, yet Jesus in **John 14**, told us we would do greater works. If He mentioned it about us, then it must be important to Him. Yet it seems to elude us.

John 5:12–20 (KJV 1900) — *12 Then asked they him, What man is that which said unto thee, Take up thy bed, and walk? 13 And he that was healed wist not who it was: for Jesus had conveyed himself away, a multitude being in that place. 14 Afterward Jesus findeth him in the temple, and said unto him, Behold, thou art made whole: sin* *no more, lest a worse thing come unto thee. 15 The man departed, and told the Jews that it was Jesus, which had made him whole. 16 And therefore did the Jews persecute Jesus, and sought to slay him, because he had done these things on the sabbath day. 17 <u>But Jesus answered them, My Father worketh hitherto, and I work</u>. 18 Therefore the Jews sought the more to kill him, because he not only had broken the sabbath, but said also that God was his Father, making himself equal with God. 19 Then answered Jesus and said unto them, Verily, verily, I say unto you, The Son can do nothing of himself, but what he seeth the Father do: for what things soever he doeth, these also doeth the Son likewise. 20 For the Father loveth the Son, and sheweth him all things that himself doeth: <u>and he will shew him greater works than these, that ye may marvel.</u>*

He said the Father was working and so He was as well. Imagine that, the Father is working! Then Jesus says that the Father would show greater works that we would marvel. So let's look at the outcome of what God desires first and that is the word 'marvel'.

Marvel means *'to wonder, have in admiration, admire, wonder at, to be wondered at, to be held in admiration'*. It comes from a root word meaning *'behold, "look'*, and *'look upon, view attentively, contemplate, to view, in the sense of visiting, meeting with a person, to learn by looking, to see with the eyes, to perceive'*.

With these definitions, it appears God indeed wants to capture us in every way. The outcome of this would be something easily seen and would hold our attention. So if it is something so visible and easy, then surely it can't be that difficult to perform. So let's begin to look in-depth to what is really being said here.

Greater comes from the Greek word meaning *'megas'* (Mega) *of number and quantity, intensity and degrees, ability and virtue, importance and relevance.*

Works comes from the Greek word *'Ergon'* meaning *'enterprise, undertaking, to work, be employed; act of labor, something accomplished by the hand, specific work an individual has been assigned to do'*.

So what is expected is for us to do a specific assignment or task that is greater in intensity, ability, and virtue. He showed the Son this!

Jesus saw something greater that the Father was actually working on or doing, then later He would convey this to His Disciples. We must see what the Father is doing and rightly perceive these things as well.

John 5:36 (KJV 1900) — *36 But I have greater witness than that of John: <u>for the works which the Father hath given me to finish, the same works that I do,</u> bear witness of me, that the Father hath sent me.*

The works Jesus was given had a conclusion and He said the Father expected Him to also finish these works. But Jesus said the witness He had sitting in these works was greater than the witness of John. Now John spoke of Jesus being the Messiah, the Chosen One, and the Greater One. What would be greater than this identity? Perhaps the nature of God itself!

To bear witness means – '*to give testimony as in a legal sense as an expert in a trial*'. These works should always bear witness to the Son. The works bear witness to the person and mission of Christ to bring men to salvation! So everything Jesus was doing was to accomplish one thing -that men would believe He was sent from the Father.

John 14:1–4 (KJV 1900) — *1 Let not your heart be troubled: ye believe in God, believe also in me. 2 In my Father's house are many mansions: if it were not so, I would have told you. I go to prepare a place for you. 3 And if I go and prepare a place for you, I will come again, and receive you unto myself; that where I am, there ye may be also. 4 And whither I go ye know, and the way ye know.*

In **John 14:12**, we see the greater works. But let's start at the beginning of the chapter and look at everything in full context. Jesus' focus of the chapter is in the first four verses. He calls for a shift in the heart because the current state of the hearts of those present is not in the right place. They are troubled which would mean they have divided affections and without strong faith or being convinced that God does have a plan. He speaks of our eternal destiny and again in vs.18, he talks about us not being orphans, but being part of a large spiritual family with an inheritance. He speaks of eternal hope as well and of a certain *way* they will find.

When we think of the word 'way', it talks of *'a pathway, a manner of life or the way a person lives'*. In essence, He is saying it's not dependent upon your heart, or your current disjointedness, or your feelings of rejection, but no matter what, you are going to find the right way of living!

John 14:8–14 (KJV 1900) — *8 Philip saith unto him, Lord, shew us the Father, and it sufficeth us. 9 Jesus saith unto him, Have I been so long time with you, and yet hast thou not known me, Philip? he that hath seen me hath seen the Father; and how sayest thou then, Shew us the Father? 10 Believest thou not that I am in the Father, and the Father in me? the words that I speak unto you I speak not of myself: <u>but the Father that dwelleth in me, he doeth the work</u>s. 11 Believe me that I am in the Father, and the Father in me: or else believe me for the very works' sake. 12 Verily, verily, I say unto you, He that believeth on me, <u>the works that I do shall he do also; and greater works than these shall he do;</u> because I go unto my Father. 13 And whatsoever ye shall ask in my name, that will I do, that the Father may be glorified in the Son. 14 If ye shall ask any*

thing in my name, I will do it.

So what are the greater works? What is this thing we seem to strive for and don't seem to attain? Is it going to be a move of God that suddenly bursts forth with dynamic moves of the Spirit? Or is this for a certain group of people or elite apostles? Was Jesus speaking to these specific apostles that they would actually do greater things than Jesus did?

Jesus started talking about believing as He spoke to Phillip. The battle always seems to be in our ability to believe. As a parent, it was easier to believe for my children than for myself. I think it is this way for most of us, but in this dialogue, the focus is upon each individual doing greater works, and it ties directly to believing. Jesus told the Pharisees that they had unbelief because they were full of themselves. They desired the accolades of men. They were full of pride. They would not let others enter in and so they were not changing their heart and embracing Jesus' new belief system. It would appear we can keep our own selves from the greater works.

John 6:28–29 (KJV 1900) — *28 Then said they unto him, What shall we do, that we*

might work the works of God? 29 Jesus answered and said unto them, This is the work of God, that ye believe on him whom he hath sent.

Jesus had already told the disciples they needed to believe ON Him, not believe they could do miracles. It is about what, where and Who our focus is on. It is not about what He gives, produces, or performs. The word 'on' means '*towards something* or *for something*'. It is a word that describes an action of the past. He said to believe or have faith of this past action that Christ was sent (*apostellos)*, to the earth. That sending was a specific function of salvation to all of humanity and the freedom and liberty from sin.

Looking at **John 14** again, let's start looking at the Disciples or Apostles. There are no records of them doing any greater miracles than Jesus. Notice, it does not say to do greater miracles, signs, wonders, healings, prophecies or visions, but to do greater works. Most people believe the works are to validate the one doing them. If we have a healing gift come into our midst, the next time we gather, we always have testimonies of those that were healed. We do this to validate the person with the healing gift, but we seldom hear validation of the message of Christ and the Resurrection. You do not hear validation of the nature of God or the breath of God that came in that moment and touched that person. But we do hear about the anointing or the action of the Holy Spirit. The reason the person has the healing gift is because they've made place within their nature to receive that healing nature of Christ, they have let it become resident within them. It is from that creative position that the person is then able to allow the gifting of the Holy Spirit to flow through them. When in reality, they are to validate the Christ! In that context, the Disciples and Apostles did do greater works. They brought more validation than Christ Himself could possible do.

But let's define exactly what is being said here. The word 'works' means '*enterprise, undertaking, to work, be employed, act of labour, something accomplished by the hand, a specific work an individual has been assigned to do*' shall we do because He is going to the Father. The definition has nothing to do with miracles or healings even though the Apostles did that. But Jesus' assignment for them was to convey the message of the Cross, Resurrection and eternal life. So the works are directly related to the Cross and Resurrection.

At the Cross, the nature of God became available to all men. The nature allows the ability to see the Father. The nature empowers us to do the work or assignment set before us with greater results. The nature allows us partnership with the Father to know His heart in deeper ways. The nature will testify through our lives and how we live them for the Son. So when He told them earlier to believe on Him, it had far greater meaning. He literally was saying "if you really do believe on Me and you will allow My nature to come upon you so your very life just as My very life would be a living example of My assignment on the earth, which was the Cross and Resurrection".

As you take an overall look at **John 5**, you will see there is a miracle. But when we look at **John 14**, we don't see a miracle. Yet both places are the only place in the Bible that talks about greater works. What is common to both passages is the work that Jesus is doing, He is delivering a message.

The greater works are not in multiple people doing miracles, even though the number of miracles occurring was greater, it still did not exceed the number of miracles that Jesus did by Himself. In **John 21:25,** it says that Jesus did multiple volumes of miracles that are not written down. There were so many in fact that the books could not contain all that He did. It's obvious from that verse that we're only seeing the highlights of the few examples of miracles that He performed upon the earth. If the greater works were truly all about miracles such as healings or signs and wonders, and the apostles were empowered to do that, wouldn't we be seeing that in the book of Acts? The gap in the book of Acts is we do not see any record of vast numbers of miracles or even all the miracles that Jesus did.

The greater works is not greater miracles. We do not see 5,000 people being fed in the book of Acts, we do not see a storm calmed and we do not see anyone walking on water. What we do see is the message being preached with the signs and wonders following which backs up that this indeed was the Christ that had authority over all things.

In **Acts 3**, we see the first miracle unfold. A man is sitting at the Gate Beautiful outside of the temple. His physical condition is keeping him from entering in and by law, he is not allowed to enter in. He is looked upon as being unclean. Peter comes up and reaches his hand out and says *"such as I have, give I thee"*. He was not just extending healing but was also extending the very nature of God towards him. The nature is full of love and compassion, forgiveness and mercy. The nature of God brought the healing to the man. In reality, what they did by bringing the message demonstrated by healing was they removed the obstacles from the man's life so he could enter the temple and have an encounter with God. This is indeed the greater work, the removing of obstacles from people's lives so they can find God face-to-face.

Peter had been preaching and continued to preach a message of salvation. Peter and John were both arrested and put in prison for the uproar and stir that they had caused. But upon their release, they were forbidden to preach Christ (the message). They're not forbidden to heal. They are not told not to do miracles. Even in that day, religious leaders and those in authority knew that it was not the healings or signs and wonders that would shift and change the course of people's beliefs. It was the message of the Christ the disciples were preaching. But they didn't realize it was the nature of God resident within them that brought them to the point of saying: **Acts 4:20 (KJV 1900) — *20 "For we cannot but speak the things which we have seen and heard."***

Not only were they delivering the message, but they were completing the assignment that was given to them of doing the greater works. You see the greater works is not about us moving in the gifts of the Holy Spirit's activity in our life. The greater works is delivering the message and freeing people from sin and bringing them into eternal destiny in the Most High God.

The miracles Jesus did were unique to Him. He opened a doorway that in most cases had never been seen before.

John 9:32 (KJV 1900) — *32 Since the world began was it not heard that any man opened the eyes of one that was born blind.*

John 15:24 (KJV 1900) — *24 If I had not done among them the works which none other man did, they had not had sin: but now have they both seen and hated both me and my Father.*

But the Disciples were also able to perform

some of the same miracles. What we don't think about is all the miracles the disciples did that Jesus never did do, at least it is not recorded of Him doing. Here are just a few of the greater works that the Apostles did:

1. They had mass salvations.
2. They made more disciples.
3. They delivered the message of Christ to the known world.
4. They established the Church.
(Jesus established twelve men.)
5. They opened spiritually blind eyes by the masses.
(Jesus was first to open physically and spiritually blind eyes.)
6. They gave spiritual life to the spiritually dead – (Jesus raised the dead – Lazarus.)
7. They saw people filled with the Holy Spirit.
8. They helped others move in the gifts of the Spirit.
9. They saw the nature of God spread from vessel to vessel.
10. They saw people live in the power of the Holy Spirit.

All of these things have one thing in common

The Breath of God

and that is not the performing of miracles or signs and wonders. It is the delivering of a message coming from the nature of Christ with the breath of God. The greater works are because of the intensity and virtue of the nature of God being released. Because of the Resurrection, we are undertaking and doing a specific work at hand.

Each person has unique "works" or message to give. Each has been assigned to deliver the message from the Father that through the Son, the world can be redeemed. The message still remains common to all for it is focused upon Christ and His nature resident within us.

The problem is we are waiting and waiting and waiting for the Holy Spirit to come and do a great work through us by using us for signs, wonders and miracles. We believe that if we attain these kinds of things, we will then come up to the place of being equal to what Christ did upon the earth. Remember, the scriptures say to do greater works. By the way we have looked at the greater works exceeding what Christ did, we soon come to a conclusion that we cannot attain or fulfill what has been said. We lose heart and never start on the journey at all.

The reality of it is the work that is set before us is to deliver the message. Every time the Apostles delivered the message, the Holy Spirit showed up. We are trying to do things backward because we refuse to deliver the message for fear of being rejected, we may be unsure of ourselves, or a variety of other reasons. No wonder Jesus told Phillip "*only believe*" to do the works.

Jesus did not leave us the Holy Spirit to enable us to do the works, even though the Holy Spirit's activity may be involved in us delivering the message, but He gave us the Holy Spirit as the final fulfillment that validates the work that we do. In other words, the Holy Spirit's activity upon the lives of those we are ministering to becomes the validation or an exclamation for the message that was delivered to them.

We all can agree that Jesus did the greatest work and that was the work of the Cross and the power of Resurrection from which all spiritual life flows. In all honesty, we cannot exceed this greatest work. But we can exceed it in being the voice of the greater work. There are more people alive on planet earth now than has been born from the beginning of time until now. The greatest harvest lies before us. The greatest work lies before us as well. If we would meditate on this for a moment of just how deep the work of the Cross is and how freeing it is for all of humanity, then realize that each of us have been given the privilege to deliver that very message to multitudes upon multitudes and tens of thousands upon thousands!

Without diminishing the Cross and its great work, the honor bestowed upon us to be the voice of this message is almost greater than the instrument of the Cross that birthed the message. Without the messenger of the work, the work would almost be in vain. Think about all the angels rejoicing when one sinner repents and comes to Christ and His Kingdom and then think about us bringing the message or being the vehicle of this uproar in heaven. Is that not a greater work than seeing a healing or a miracle occur before us?

You can do the greater work by learning the Gospel and learning how to explain and stand down the arguments against it. You can do the greater work by truly just believing God for everything in your life and coming under His Lordship. The Gospel message is the power of God to salvation.

- If all of us (those who are called by God) discipled one person a year, the whole world would have the potential of being saved within 20 years.
- If only a hundred million Christians (10%) would disciple one person each year, this turns to 200 million in the first year- then it multiplies to four hundred million the second year- eight hundred million in three years!
- Then on the fourth year to one and half billion- to three billion on the fifth year, to six billion in the sixth year. And that is if we disciple only one person a year!

It's obvious we have a problem with timidity and confidence that the message will do what Jesus said it would. We are told that the Lord has not given us a spirit of fear but one of power (a sign of being filled with the Spirit), courage, love, (a loving care for those unsaved) and a sound mind (one who is able to think through the arguments to refute them Biblically). The Church would be far more successful in God's eyes if we did the works He called us to!

The message is the greater work --- millions of people saved, billions!

His Nature Formed - His Breath Released

Chapter 11

Seven Fold Spirit or Graces

Isaiah 11:1–4 (KJV 1900) — *1 And there shall come forth a rod out of the stem of Jesse, And a Branch shall grow out of his roots: 2 And the spirit of the LORD shall rest upon him, The spirit of wisdom and understanding, The spirit of counsel and might, The spirit of knowledge and of the fear of the LORD; 3 And shall make him of quick understanding in the fear of the LORD: And he shall not judge after the sight of his eyes, Neither reprove after the hearing of his ears: 4 But with righteousness shall he judge the poor, And reprove with equity for the meek of the earth: And he shall smite the earth with the rod of his mouth, And with the breath of his lips shall he slay the wicked.*

I want to briefly cover the seven graces we see here in **Isaiah 11**. We normally speak of these as the seven spirits of Christ. The word 'spirit' here actually means '*breath*'. It is actually seven breaths that are resting on the nature of Christ. You see how important it is for us to truly have the nature of Christ first so then His breath can come forth out of that nature. The nature is like the resting ground for the breath.

But this is more than seven types or natures of Christ. It's actually seven breaths that get released or flow out of the nature of Christ. They are actually seven dynamics of the nature of God that release seven graces of God to produce change that carry seven breaths of God.

Revelation 1:4–5 (KJV 1900) — *4 John to the seven churches which are in Asia: Grace be unto you, and peace, from him which is, and which was, and which is to come; and <u>from the seven Spirits which are before his throne</u>; 5 And from Jesus Christ, who is the faithful witness, and the first begotten of the dead, and the prince of the kings of the earth. Unto him that loved us, and washed us from our sins in his own blood,*

Revelation 3:1 (KJV 1900) — *1 And unto the angel of the church in Sardis write; These things saith he <u>that hath</u> the seven Spirits of God, and the seven stars; I know thy works, that thou hast a name that thou* *livest, and art dead.*

The throne is the stationary place of authority, non-changing and everlasting. I love how everything in heaven evolves and is in motion around the throne. These seven spirits we see here are before the throne. The word 'before' means *'to be present in his sight'*. It comes from two words meaning *'in a fixed position to be seen'*. The word 'spirit', in the shortest definition, means *'breath'*. So it actually can mean there are seven breaths of God in a fixed position being constantly seen and looked upon by God upon the throne!

Rev. 3:1 shows these breaths can be possessed and refers to Jesus possessing these. The nature of Christ has several distinct breaths that create dynamics of life. So, as Jesus possessed these breaths, the eye of the Father was upon Him! He was peering down and seeing how Jesus would steward these breaths. What would go into motion? Who would be touched? Now that is really deep! These things are about the ways of God that we don't even comprehend exist.

What I find amazing is the fact that the seven

breaths are constantly before the throne but are also resident within the nature of Christ within us upon the Earth. Just like the nature of God can be resident both in heaven and upon the earth, so can His breath as well. It's as if His nature dwelling within us connects us with His Spirit. And His breath flowing out of us connects His intentions into the earth. When we speak with the breath of God, we have loosed all of heaven to back up what we have said because we have spoken as if God was speaking to Himself.

Matthew 16:18–19 (KJV 1900) — *18 And I say also unto thee, That thou art Peter, and upon this rock I will build my church; and the gates of hell shall not prevail against it. 19 And I will give unto thee the keys of the kingdom of heaven: and whatsoever thou shalt bind on earth shall be bound in heaven: and whatsoever thou shalt loose on earth shall be loosed in heaven.*

No wonder that Jesus said that whatsoever you bind on the earth is bound in heaven and whatsoever you loose on the earth is loosed in heaven. He was not only talking about binding and loosing demonic forces and freedom and

The Breath of God

liberty, but He was talking about binding or stopping the breath of God from coming and also loosening or allowing the breath of God to flow. He was talking about stopping or loosing the nature of God within to release the breath without. When Peter spoke the revelation to Jesus about who He was, the only way he knew was his spirit had connected to the nature of God and the words that came forth were the breath of God.

Jesus was talking about what the keys of heaven were. He was talking about what would open or create an access point into all of heaven and what would stop this access point as well. The breath of God is one of those keys that unlocks all of eternity. It's as if when we loose the breath of God that we open a doorway or portal of heaven, that heaven and all of its resources can come down upon the Earth!

He essentially told Peter that he had discovered the "unlock system of heaven". It was not the revelation of Jesus being the Christ, even though that was part of it. It was what occurred behind the scenes that Jesus was excited about. He didn't say "Great revelation!" but was focused on how the revelation came. The nature of God had connected with the nature of Peter and revealed the Christ. After all, Peter had been told and knew He was the Christ. He probably had told many people about it. But now his spirit was convinced of it and had no choice but to let the breath come forth and speak it.

2 Timothy 3:16 (KJV 1900) — *16 All scripture is given by inspiration of God, and is profitable for doctrine, for reproof, for correction, for instruction in righteousness:*

2 Peter 1:21 (KJV 1900) — *21 For the prophecy came not in old time by the will of man: but holy men of God spake as they were moved by the Holy Ghost.*

You see the whole Bible is inspired and is the breath of God. God's breath was coming through them. It is alive in the pages and leaps out to us to create in us. That's why the word will not return void. It can do nothing but produce life. It is up to us to steward this life thus stewarding the breath of God.

These men and women spoke as if God was

speaking. This is why we look at them today, study them and desire to be like them. But the same Spirit is still writing the New Testament today, still breathing the freshness of God forth, and still creating both the future and past in the same moment. It is a glorious thing to be highly cherished that God would speak through us in such degrees of revealing glory. Such hidden treasures and such responsibility upon our lives and especially from our lips!

This is why we must be careful in what we say. Our faith is always active and always coming into agreement with something. What we hear seems to be what our faith gets activated on most. But what we say can also carry the same weight of glory and put things into motion. Perhaps our lips and words are carrying a far more exceeding weight of Glory than we realize. Perhaps they are carrying the breath to degrees in which we are unaware.

I know this to be a fact in my own life. In ministry, you have so many conversations with people. Some are official and some not so official and some just casual and others still are a mixture. What I have experienced is to give direction or advice coming from an official place and others were in a casual place.

The things I said were not taken seriously at the time so later on, because of failure to do, or respond, or act, the lack came back to have consequences. I soon realized it does not matter whether the conversations were 'official or unofficial', words have power and when in a leadership role, they can carry God's breath as well. We need to heed what we say and how we respond.

We call them the seven fold anointing of Christ found in *Isaiah 11:1-3.* But in reality they are not truly anointings, nor are they gifting. Anointings are to meet a specific need present and are not dependent upon the state of the person moving under that anointing. Anyone can be anointed even an ass was anointed and spoke. The same with gifting. Giftings are divided to several as the Spirit wills. All can prophesy and move in the gifts of the Spirit. So to look at the seven spirits of **Isaiah 11:1** and say they are anointings or gifting diminishes the dynamic of what these seven breaths really mean.

When the breath of God comes, it has the ability to create changes. This is not a onetime event but sets something in motion of ongoing

The Breath of God

change. In other words, these seven spirits or breaths are actually seven graces of Christ (the already anointed one) the Messiah (gift given) carried. It was not the fullness of an anointing or divine enablement, even though that was always present, but was an actual grace. This is not a saving grace which most of us equate with grace. Nor is it a keeping grace or a grace that means *favor*, even though that is how we have interpreted grace and done the word a great injustice. The word 'grace' actually means *'change be it good or bad'*. It is an ability to bring shift where needed, confront what is needed and set the course for a fresh new thing. As Jesus, Paul, Peter, Timothy and others moved in these breaths and set things in motion, the eye of the Father was upon them as well. The outcome people revived was "favor" with God. But what was required to see this was "change" that someone had to implement and many times was not well received. One is real grace and the other is the benefit of grace.

Anyone can be anointed. Anyone can have a gift flow through them. Both are generally towards individuals. What I am talking about is a grace that is for the corporate body! Paul said in **Ephesians 3:1** that he had been given a dispensation of grace or a stewardship of grace. If he is talking about salvation grace then Paul would be determining who would be saved. Paul was talking about how he released and stewarded the graces upon his life.

Grace is the expression of your relationship with God. It shows forth the degree of change that you have allowed to occur in your life. Every day we are stewarding the grace that is upon our life. Every situation in life that comes along is creating decision points that we determine how we will respond. Many times the responses require change either in our lives or the lives of others. That's why Paul knew that his words were powerful and had to be chosen wisely. They carried the ability to bring change into the lives of all those around him. When people looked to Paul's life, they were also looking at the grace that was resting upon him. They're actually seeing how he conducted his life and stewarded the great mysteries of God.

Actually grace is also the pathway of how holiness is expressed to others. Holiness is not expressed through gifts or anointings. If holiness was determined by anointings upon a person's life or how well they moved in gifting, then we would not see some of the failures we have experienced in the leadership of the Church. Our misconception that anointing equals character or holiness has diminished what real character in holiness is. But when holiness is sustained in lives, we can then begin to see the fullness of grace or one of the seven fold breaths of God begin to be truly established.

The deepest relationship we can have is a relationship of holiness before God. It is actually the foundation in the essence of God. By God's holiness, all creation was spoken into existence in the same way the seven graces that we see in **Isaiah 11** are also directly connected to holiness. As God breathes with His Spirit upon us, His breath is connected with holiness as well. In all honesty, grace comes upon our life creating change in the changes to bring us into a more holy state before God.

Isaiah 11:1–3 (KJV 1900) — *1 And there shall come forth a rod out of the stem of Jesse, And a Branch shall grow out of his roots:*

2 And the spirit of the Lord shall rest upon him, The spirit of wisdom and understanding, The spirit of counsel and might, The spirit of knowledge and of the fear of the Lord; 3 And shall make him of quick understanding in the fear of the Lord: And he shall not judge after the sight of his eyes, Neither reprove after the hearing of his ears:

SPIRIT OF THE LORD

For the most part, much of the Church is in the first breath or the place of "***the Spirit of the Lord is upon me***". This breath or grace is the place of salvation and deliverance. If you are a believer, then you have received this breath upon your life. The breath that we bring forth out of our spirit from this experience is telling others of the great salvation that we experienced in the great freedom and deliverance that occurred in our life. The excitement of sharing the joy of our salvation comes with a tremendous zeal and passion. It captivates the listeners as we tell our story and unfold redemption's plan.

This breath also carries a tremendous grace to

share our faith with it. What is happening in this grace is the Lordship of Christ is being developed in an individual. This is the place the realities of what we call Biblical world view principles are formed. There are four principles that set the course for our belief system that all things flow from:

1. Knowing God as creator
2. He is Lord of that creation
3. He is sovereign
4. He is providential.

We may not understand these four things in detail but we are experiencing an underlying principle. In many ways, these four things become the message of the new believer as he tries to convey the grace that he is participating in.

This is a grace that shifts us into a true understanding that we are eternal beings with eternal purposes to be exercised by our lives. Without this first grace developed, we will lack community and connectedness with a body of believers. We will break covenant with those we walk with. We will abandon the promises given us and settle for the typical Christian lifestyle. We will not have ourselves being used by God.

But if we truly embrace this breath to come into our lives, it will touch every hidden corner just like a wind can get into every crevasse of our heart. This grace settles identity. This is the place we see ourselves as a gift to others and that God has anointed us to be that gift. It settles not just who we are but what our primary assignments are. This grace gives us access not just for forgiveness, the beginning stages, but to be holy, the finished stages. It is a grace that gives us the greatest advantage point. It is a partnership that is covenantal with the Lord and others.

When Jesus stood in **Luke 4:18** and declared the Spirit of the Lord was upon Him, He stated that God had consumed Him in this breath and grace. He knew His assignment. He knew His purpose. His identity was settled. Eternity was bearing down upon Him. He and the Lord (Jehovah, the all existing One) were in a total partnership. He was His representative upon the earth. This first grace and the last, the fear of the Lord, are key to unlocking those remaining. Without Alpha and Omega, we will never see the others. We will now jump to the last one as without it, we will never be able to move fully in the other five graces listed or receive the breath associated with them as it comes.

The fear of the Lord is the other bookend that holds the rest of the graces in place. With the true Spirit of the Lord on one end and the Spirit of the fear of the Lord on the other end, we end up with an open ended belief system. We can either ponder a belief system that is open ended in grace because "I'm a child of God and all things being justified" or we end up in a belief system that is fear based and works driven. At times, we end up having the other graces in between trying to move into our lives but are not truly effective because we've not placed these two boundaries into existence. Thus God cannot allow these other graces or breaths from Him to come in fullness or it would be like trying to pour water into a container that has no bottom or sides.

Isaiah 11:1–3 (KJV 1900) — *1 And there shall come forth a rod out of the stem of Jesse, And a Branch shall grow out of his roots: 2 And the spirit of the Lord shall rest upon him, The spirit of wisdom and understanding, The spirit of counsel and might, The spirit of knowledge and of the* *fear of the Lord; 3 And shall make him of quick understanding in the fear of the Lord: And he shall not judge after the sight of his eyes, Neither reprove after the hearing of his ears:*

The verse above also says that God wants to bring a quick understanding of this grace of the fear of the Lord. For God to add that in the description and focus upon only this one, it holds a great importance and key. The fear of the Lord is not terror or dread. Nor is it even an emotional response of surprise, etc. It is a holy reverence for God because of the awesomeness of seeing Him for who He truly is. This ability to see comes from the depth of holy reverence and respect and recognition of Him, *the Spirit of the Lord is upon me*. The awe of God allows us to see who we really are and what we have been redeemed from. It brings great humility with it as well. A servant's heart is formed by having the fear of the Lord and without this; the other five graces will not really operate. This is the place obedience comes from.

This is not obedience by forced actions to be accepted or to feel approval but because of heart condition and reverence. The fear of the Lord is His delight says **Isaiah 3:3**. God does not delight in our terror of Him but our respect of Him. It is what brings heartfelt repentance and an ongoing heart examination to see if our condition is right. Without the fear of the Lord, people will live a mixed life and allow worldly things to be part of their makeup. We see much of this in Christian life as we have lost our reverence and awe of God. Proverbs also says this "fear "will lead us to wisdom. It is not human wisdom that Proverbs is talking about but the grace of wisdom, the seven fold breath of wisdom.

This "breath of awe" comes down upon us and as it does so, it brings a portion of heaven with it. It is like a portal placed upon our heart to treasure the eternal realm and thus we safeguard it. Without this in place, we will never truly cherish the other graces as they come upon us. This second breath of the fear of the Lord is the breath now coming upon the Church. It is the breath that causes decisions and long term commitments to the assignments. It causes a resolve in current and future covenants. It causes a great strength to come forth upon those who breathe this breath in and allow it to come upon them. It also shifts us from having no natural fear of rejection, men opinions, and failure. It brings a convincing of complete victory and overcoming obstacles because of the awe of knowing the one who sits upon the throne.

This shift allows the other graces to move freely and have their full effect as they bear down upon humanity. Faith is released through the other graces in full potential and impact. The fear of the Lord is also an element that needs to be in place as it causes great faith to arise for the future and the assignments of the Lord.

There have been times the presence of the Lord has visited me and great awe was upon me as I literally hid from God. On one occasion, it was the middle of the night and I was in a deep sleep. The Holy Spirit was speaking to me about many of the things of God. Suddenly I was awakened by the Spirit of the Lord and was fully alert. I was also very aware of holiness from those encompassing my bedroom. It was as if the room was lit in a very light that I could see with my spirit but was not evident to the natural eye. I knew God

The Breath of God

was standing in the corner peering upon me. I was overwhelmed with His Holiness and even though I knew that I was in right standing and clean before Him, I felt that I was still not in the right position to even peer at Him. It was as if I drew back and I took the bed covers and pulled them over my head. Without any words being spoken, I could sense a tremendous impartation of the holiness of God encompassing me and giving me specific deposits. I felt so unworthy in the moment and I continued to hide myself. After about twenty-five minutes of this visitation, I could sense the presence of God had moved out of the room and was no longer standing peering upon me. But the residue of His presence remained for almost two hours. I was frozen in awe and the fear of God and didn't move from under the covers the whole time. That is what the fear of God is truly like.

Isaiah had this experience in **Isaiah 6** as he sees himself as undone and a man of unclean lips. He saw that unless God determined he had come to the true point of reverence for Him, that he could not carry the breath God wanted to give Him. The Spirit of the fear of the Lord would release the other graces for

Isaiah specifically, wisdom, understanding and might. Without the fear of the Lord, these graces would not be released. It would take the awe of God to truly understand wisdom and understanding and to steward them properly. God pronounced him clean and in that pronouncement, he received the breath of those graces!

We also see Paul in his encounter on the Damascus road being confronted and having Godly fear. The outcome was God healed Paul's physical eyes, which is a type and shadow of his spiritual sight. Paul stepped into the breath and grace of the eyes of his understanding being enlightened. This breath upon Paul's life would forever change him. He saw the advantage of receiving the Spirit's breath upon him. He would write about it to the Ephesus Church to release those graces that would create change upon them.

Ephesians 1:17–23 (KJV 1900) — *That the God of our Lord Jesus Christ, the <u>Father of glory</u>, may give unto you the spirit of <u>wisdom</u> and <u>revelation</u> in the <u>knowledge</u> of him: 18 <u>The eyes of your understanding being enlightened;</u> that ye may know what* *is the hope of his calling, and what the riches of the glory of his inheritance in the saints, 19 And what is the exceeding greatness of his <u>power</u> to us-ward who believe, according to the working of his mighty power, 20 Which he wrought in Christ, when he raised him from the dead, and set him at his own right hand in the heavenly places, 21 Far above all principality, and power, and might, and dominion, and every name that is named, not only in this world, but also in that which is to come: 22 And hath put all things under his feet, and gave him to be the head over all things to the church, 23 Which is his body, the fulness of him that filleth all in all.*

This again is not natural understanding but the spirit of understanding. The breath of understanding. Paul knew instantly the time and season of God and stepped into the functioning of those needed graces. I believe each person has certain graces assigned to them at birth to be engaged in through life. It is God's plan of success for us.

Now with the Spirit of the Lord and the Spirit

of fear of the Lord in place, we will look at the rest of the graces or breaths of God that come with His nature.

Isaiah 11: 2 *And the spirit of the LORD shall rest upon him, The spirit of wisdom and understanding, The spirit of counsel and might, The spirit of knowledge and of the fear of the LORD;*

SPIRIT OF WISDOM

Let's now look at the Spirit or breath of wisdom. The wisdom of God then becomes the experience or sum total of God's understanding. Now in all reality, we move in parts of that but in no means the fullness of it. The spirit of wisdom is seen in how we act out our lives before others. It is the reflection of our heart and what we truly believe. It is the place we make choices and decisions. We either believe God is victorious and can gain victory in all things or our lives will reflect the areas we don't believe God has this power. It is also the place confidence comes from for the implementation of promises and prophetic words God has given us. We generally describe this grace this way: as life experience gained to be shared with others. In reality, that is what is produced after this grace has been allowed to function in a person's life for a season.

Natural wisdom or intellectualism is the furthest thing from the breath of God that comes from the Throne in wisdom. With natural wisdom, we can build anything. The Tower of Babel is a good example of this as God said "Man could do anything his mind was set upon". We also see this in the development of society, medicine, science, etc. For the most part today, we think people have wisdom as they have built large ministries but a good administrator can do that. How many large ministries are making a skillful advance of bringing the Kingdom of God into the earth to change the course of societies and cultures? Yet this is what Jesus did. This is what Paul and many others did.

The word 'wisdom' here in Hebrew means *'spiritual skill for war or advancement".* It is what we act out before others in our choices and how we receive instruction. Wisdom is the place where both teaching and revelatory gifting comes from. Since revelation is deeper than doctrinal understanding, it requires wisdom to know how to correctly interpret and apply what is being given. I see a lot of people wanting revelation but lack the breath of wisdom so when revelation does come, it comes out almost making no sense or no real way to connect the dots.

The spirit of wisdom is also the place revelation comes from in a way. It is the connectedness revelation needs to be most efficient. It is the reason revelation comes and is needed. It is needed by teachers and other five-fold ministry gifts as they must not only know the times and seasons (spirit of knowledge) but what to do in that season (spirit of wisdom) to effectively equip the saints. It is the plan of God to be implemented upon the earth that all others things revolve around.

This is where the grace with wisdom must be applied. Since grace is the ability to create change, the breath of wisdom comes to create change in both our understanding and the application of it to create life experience. Revelation that comes must first be applied within the person's life for this grace to become wisdom. Once voiced, it becomes revelation to others that they too, must embrace the grace with it and let the same process come to fullness in them.

The Breath of God

This is a grace that intercessors, ministry leaders and missionaries require. It is required by apostles to strategize and implement plans of advancement. It also is where counseling of other ministers and giving ministry advice is drawn from.

This grace is the grace to receive the large plan of God. It is the rally call to come around and implement. Most are not willing to submit themselves to this nor do they desire it. The lack of instruction from the source of change is hurting the advancement of the Kingdom. Without this breath allowed to function, the Body becomes disjointed. People abandon their post and lose heart in what God has promised.

Spiritual fathering also requires this breath and without it, nothing more than discipleship is going to occur. Spiritual fathering requires having vision for what a person will become (wisdom applied in their life) and then knowing how to bring that person into the revelations needed to have wisdom and life experience to firmly be a part of their life.

The outcome of the spirit of wisdom is not only is a person walking in this grace but also is carrying the breath of this. A nature of wisdom has been established. This is not measured by how many are following, or gathering, even though that might play into it, but about the decree of influence and impact that is made when the person speaks. It is more about the depth coming from the nature than outward signs of numbers of people gathered as a sign of affirmation or approval. Generally the greatest revelation in the spirit of wisdom and this portion of the nature of Christ, will divide more than gather. Things will be said that seem hard to understand and may force people to make decisions regarding the direction of their lives.

Proverbs 24:3-4 (KJV 1900) — *3 Through wisdom is an house builded; And by understanding it is established: 4 And by knowledge shall the chambers be filled With all precious and pleasant riches.*

This wisdom will build the house or people of God. All apostles must move in this apostolic dynamic and nature of Christ. Apostles are called to be wise master builders. This is why all apostles are spiritual fathers but not all spiritual fathers are apostles. Just as apostles are '*sent ones*', so are revelation and wisdom sent. They come to set the course for the future.

This is not the same as the gift of the Spirit in **1 Corinthians 12**. The word of wisdom or knowledge is a singular word for a singular situation. The spirit of wisdom and knowledge is a nature, a grace, a breath, the forming of a certain lifestyle that reflects another ongoing dynamic of Christ.

SPIRIT OF UNDERSTANDING

Proverbs says the house will be established with understanding. The word 'understanding' in the Hebrew means '*to perceive or discern by the spirit*'. It is not intuition or speculation but actually true discernment and spiritual perception. This grace upon the Church creates the Body of Christ to be one in heart and mind. It is the place in which true fellowship is developed and a spiritual community begins to be formed. It is where the oneness of **John 17** starts to come into focus, to be one in Name, one in Word, to be one in glory, and one in perfection.

The spirit of understanding is different that

the spirit of wisdom. As wisdom is the plan of advancement, the spirit of understanding means *'to perceive and to discern by the spirit'*. It is the place of rightly dividing the word of truth and the intentions and motives that people display. It is the knowing in the spirit that goes beyond what you see with your natural eyes and hear with your natural ears. It is the place that true covenants are made between people, vision for others and their gifting is put in place and real community is formed with purpose.

The breath of understanding is also required to lead gatherings into fullness. It is the fusing together of a people to be one heart and mind containing one passion and desire. It is the motive behind the instruction of the saints. It is to be protected and moves to hold true doctrine in place, and moves in discipline and correction when necessary. If a person lacks in any of these then the spirit of understanding is lacking.

It was breathed out at Pentecost as they, as a community, had discernment and covenantal purpose. It was not so much the speaking in tongues that was the miracle, even though you never dismiss anything supernatural. The miracle was the seven fold nature of Christ and the breath of God to come and blow these graces into the Church. It was what launched the early Church to be fully dynamic. The Body of Christ had discernment of what needed to be said and done and also perceived their role in bringing the Kingdom of God into the Earth. When the outpouring came, the spirit of understanding came as well.

Without all these parameters in place, the other breaths or graces have only a small impact. Most people right now have the Spirit of the Lord, are coming into the spirit of fear of the Lord, and a handful of forerunners are in the spirit of understanding. You see this grace requires you to stand where others will not stand. To remain standing when others abandon, and to eventually pull others up into the place you're standing so you can move on to other assignments.

The spirit of understanding is one of the greatest advantages as it multiples the other six giftings. It even deepens the Spirit of the Lord and the spirit of the fear of the Lord. It brings great perception to the other graces. It allows the other graces to connect to purpose and motive. It keeps hearts in check before the

Lord. It reveals wrong purposes and agendas as well. Without the spirit of understanding, wrong or mixed doctrine is birthed, functions are lacking and people are not developed in gift and calling. Overall, the Body is fragmented.

This breath and grace of God requires us to go deeper, to the point where deep calls unto deep (extreme to extreme). This is the place we truly know the intentions of the Father and we become partners in safeguarding His heart.

But this grace has an ability to connect joint to joint. What most do not understand in all these graces is that when they "move on" from a body that is functioning in these, they are abandoning the grace upon that group. Thus like Paul said, they frustrate the grace and make it ineffective. This is why some receive from a group or body because of the grace they stepped into. They then try to find grace in other groups where it might not be active or even be released. A person should find the grace upon a group and then engage in that grace. Even if it requires them to leave soul ties and structures carrying no life to a structure that has life.

The Breath of God

The fire of God and passion of God is in the spirit of understanding. Once our perception of the things of God is awakened, the fire of God and the passion of God come as well. If we are lacking the fire and the drive, then we are lacking the breath of understanding.

This grace upon the Church enables the house to be established. This is the place of perfecting the saints for the work of the ministry. It is not just instruction but heartfelt impartation of spirit to Spirit.

All apostles and teachers must have the spirit of understanding to be effective in ministry. We are not building a natural way or establishing by programs, but we are establishing the things of the Spirit deep in the spirits of people. I believe Jesus breathed on His disciples to receive the Holy Spirit in **John 20** that they received the nature of Christ to understand the spiritual importance of that moment of time. They received the nature of this spirit and grace gift. It moved them to the Upper Room to see the full manifestation of this grace which was poured out at Pentecost.

THE SPIRIT OF COUNSEL

The next gift we will look at is the spirit of

counsel. The word 'counsel' means *'a purpose that has been devised, advice, or guidance'*. This is a spiritual nature that is beyond humanistic counseling of the soul and emotions. This is counseling the spirit within a person.

This is what causes us to know the plans and intentions of God and how to implement them into the earth. It is not an action but an actual nature we can have. It is the place that teams of ministers are formed from and the promises of God are beginning to be seen coming from, birthing to maturity.

With this grace, a worship leader can move into the prophetic veins of God's creative flow. Most of the songs that come prophetically are songs of God's counseling nature. Prophets who utter God's prophetic voice must have this grace and breath flowing in their lives. It is the breath that causes a prophet to speak a word not to an individual but to a region that shifts the region. The counsel of God will be heard, seen and felt through these types of prophetic utterances.

For pastors that move in this breath, the ability to resolve the issues quickly in people's lives is present. It's not counseling that comes

The Breath of God

by mere observation or even dialogue. This counseling does not speak to the symptoms that we see but specifically addresses the root issue that is hidden that no one has even declared. It is counsel that not only sets direction for the moment but sets the future in motion.

It is also a grace that is required for those doing deliverance upon those plagued with demonic influence or possession. But probably the main place that we see the greatest need for this grace and breath to flow and nature to be formed, is in anyone in the role of leading a gathering of people. To know the flow of God and that the Spirit is beckoning in the moment of time as it unfolds, is critical to people having true encounters through the Holy Spirit with the God of the universe. Some people leading meetings seem to not know when there's been a spiritual shift or the need for the shift to occur. They continue on in a pattern to be sure that a certain task was accomplished when in reality, it may not have been. They may not know when to make the change in the meeting or when to continue a certain vein that is unfolding or how to correct it when a turn seems to have been missed in the spiritual flow. They are either not living in the grace and breath of the spirit of counsel or never truly received.

People with the spirit of counsel are able to say one line statements that carry extreme weight and great hidden revelation. It is not coming by eloquent speech but by the spirit of counsel. It is much like what Solomon operated in that the leaders of other kingdoms came to hear.

A great example that has always held with me is by a man that very few know called Arthur Burt. When he was asked about the next move of God coming and if we were ready for it, his response was, God says, *"I can do more with the less because of the Greater"*. The spirit of counsel has the ability to stop conversations and cause people to look deep in their spirit about what was just said.

THE SPIRIT OF MIGHT

The breath of might is a much needed nature we can sure use a lot of. The word 'might' in Hebrew means *'force, bravery, mighty acts and deeds'*. The spirit of might is beyond our human strength and abilities.

It is the place the Spirit of God is released

The Breath of God

through the working and manifestation of great signs and wonders. It is where boldness comes from that enables us to go forth and proclaim and demonstrate the Kingdom of God. There is a special grace that is beyond us moving in just an anointing, or an enablement of the Spirit. This is the place where the Spirit of the Lord leads us, not just on an adventure that has no meaning, but on a manifestation and demonstration of the Kingdom. This is where we go forward in confident faith overcoming all obstacles in opposition and facing those things which we have never faced before in our life. It is the place where we make decrees. It is the place where we confront principalities and powers and demonic forces. It is the place of fearlessness and overcoming ability to confront anything that is in front of us because the nature of might is so much stronger than our human nature or desires.

I remember when I was in Nigeria, in the main city, Lagos, late on a Saturday night. That is definitely not a place you want to be at that time of day. We were caught in a major traffic jam and all the power was out so there were no streetlights or house lights anywhere. We had just left a service and were traveling back to our motel. A man approached and poked his head into our car window along with a handgun. He said "I'm a robber; give me all your money!" The four of us in the car did not say a word, nor look at each other, but we all simply stared at him. You could sense the spirit of fear swirling inside the car trying to find a person that would embrace it and then it could light upon them. When none of us embraced that fear, we could visibly see it return upon the man himself. He started shaking and eventually took off running down the street. Not one of us had said a single word. That was the spirit of might or the nature of the might of God resting upon us. The breath or nature of the spirit of might carries with it a special grace; it gives us the enablement to face martyrdom in situations that put our life in peril. It is also the place of greatest reward, and seeing God move in the greatest ways. Throughout history there have been men that were graced with this special grace and nature of God. The spirit of might comes to vessels that have died to self and selfish ambitions. The spirit of might also comes to those who have no concern for worldly gain or the affections and accolades that people would bring them. The spirit of might is a special grace that causes the activation of the creativity of God and sees the breath of God be manifest in the Earth. It brings results when results can be brought no other way.

THE SPIRIT OF KNOWLEDGE

The spirit of knowledge is not intellect, or intellectual assent, or human reasoning but goes beyond how we even define the word 'knowledge'. Knowledge in Hebrew means '*the cunning ability to know the intentions*'. It means '*to know the times and seasons of God and what to do in those moments'.* Not only is it the nature of God, but it is also a special grace that enables a person to hold fast to the promises they have received until they are fully manifest.

 By knowing the times and seasons, a person is not discouraged as they know that all things said will surely come to pass. It is also the ability to discern between spirits and what is clean and unclean. It is to know the real intentions behind a person's motive and actions.

This grace has the ability to rightly divide the Word of God as well. You cannot have the spirit of knowledge without the fear of the

Lord because without Godly fear, knowledge puffs up. Without the fear of the Lord, knowledge will kill the life flow of God as a person eats from the tree of knowledge and not the tree of life. This spirit of knowledge is the tree of life. The spirit of knowledge of knowing the intentions and times and seasons has an effect on all of the other spirits of the Lord.

But probably the greatest thing the nature of knowledge does is that when applied to all the other graces, it has a supernatural ability to multiply the effectiveness of each. You see, when you know the intentions of wisdom or counsel or might or understanding, those others graces then are more effective. Teachers are very key to have this nature deep within them as well as evangelists. Really, all ministry graces need this discernment that comes by the Spirit.

You see, the Spirit knows what truth needs to be applied in each situation not by intellectual knowledge but coming from the nature of knowledge.

The seven spirits of the Lord or graces are the only true graces that will remain when all things have failed. The seven graces are what

The Breath of God

the Lord is endeavoring to do in building community amongst His people. The seven spirits of the Lord or seven graces are also the seven natures of God. They are not only descriptive but reveal function as well.

These seven graces allow our limitations to be removed once we are clothed with them. Jesus wore the seven graces as a garment, as a coat of many colors that was woven by the hand of God into His very life and existence. The woman with the issue of blood reached out and touched the hem of His garment. She was actually touching the undergarment of Jesus as it hung down. The undergarment was a garment that was woven out of one single-strand and was the hidden covering covered by an outer garment.

These graces are coming upon the Church or in the hidden place that not many see. They are forming a single garment or mantle that we are to be wearing, the very nature of the Lord. When we begin to wear these breaths of God as part of our life, it will be attractive to those that are in need and they will reach out toward us to have that touch that can heal and set them free. Let us endeavor not just to seek after the gifts of the Spirit but begin to pursue the seven spirits, the seven breaths, and the seven graces of the Lord.

Seven Breaths/Natures/Graces Overview

Isaiah 11:1–3 (KJV 1900) — 1 And there shall come forth a rod out of the stem of Jesse, And a Branch shall grow out of his roots: 2 And the spirit of the LORD shall rest upon him, The spirit of wisdom and understanding, The spirit of counsel and might, The spirit of knowledge and of the fear of the LORD; 3 And shall make him of quick understanding in the fear of the LORD: And he shall not judge after the sight of his eyes, Neither reprove after the hearing of his ears:

Seven fold Spirit of God --- not Christ

Christ possessed these spirits but they are part of the Throne room as well.

These are <u>not seven primary giftings,</u> they are more than that.

- o Gifting is something given to everyone.
- o Gifting is something that comes easily or naturally.

The Breath of God

These are <u>not seven primary anointings</u> but they are more than that.

- Anointings are a divine enablement.
- Anointings are to meet a specific need that is present.
- Anointings are not dependent upon the state of a person.

These are seven states of grace.

- Grace is a state of favor that rests and does not disappear.
- Grace is a position given to steward.
- Grace is the ability of God to bring change.
- **Grace is the expression of our relationship with God.**
- These "Graces "are how holiness is expressed.
- <u>These are all associated with power --- holiness is what empowers each Grace.</u>
- <u>Holiness is a sustained relationship with the Lord that allows grace to fully flow.</u>

- From that relationship of grace, we have a flow of gifting.
- From that relationship of grace, we have a flow of anointings.

The deepest relationship is a relationship:

- of holiness, ---- the foundation, the essence of God
- by holiness --- the function of God's seven graces
- in holiness --- the state of existence created by seven graces

The first and last of the seven spirits is required to embrace the rest.

These are knitted graces that form a garment that Christ wore.
These are transforming graces for the corporate man.

The Seven Graces To Form a Mantle

- **<u>Spirit (Breath) of the Lord</u>** --- His presence --- Spirit breath
    - Lord = the one true name of God, Jehovah, the existing one, salvation
    - The Lordship -- opens at salvation
    - The Lord of Hosts – the removal of demonic influences to receive Christ
    - The creator --- the act of salvation to regenerate
    - The sovereignty of God – the freedom of God to work in our lives for salvation
    - This is the main grace evangelists operate in.
    - It means we have stepped into a grace that allows us to be eternal beings!
        - This gives us an advantage point.

- **<u>Spirit (Breath) of wisdom</u>** --- His life (experience)

- Wisdom = spiritual skill for war or advancement
- What we act out before others
- Make choices
- Build ministries
- The place of instruction
    - The place of teaching and revelatory gifting are released
- This is a grace that intercessors, ministry leaders and missionaries require.

- **<u>Spirit (Breath) of understanding</u>** --- revelation --
  - Understanding = to perceive or discern by the Spirit
  - To be one in heart and mind
  - Place that true fellowship is made, unity
  - The fire of God and passion of God is in the spirit of understanding.
    - If lacking, then lacking understanding
  - This is the place of perfecting the saints for ministry.

- Not by instruction (wisdom) but by heartfelt spirit to Spirit.
- The spirit of understanding is required by all apostles and teachers.
- I believe Jesus breathing on His disciples to receive the Holy Spirit was the release of the spirit of understanding. It moved them to the Upper Room to see the full manifestation of this grace which was poured out at Pentecost.

- **<u>Spirit (Breath) of Counsel</u>** ---- beyond human reason
  - Counsel = purpose devised, advice
  - Being of like faith, guidance,
  - The oneness Jesus spoke of in **John 17**
  - To know what pleases God
  - Place prayer is formed
  - Place team ministry is formed

- This is the place the promises of God are birthed.
- This is required by prophets to step into and live in the counsel of God.
- This is required by pastors who counsel individuals.
- This is required by those doing deliverance.
- This is also required by those who can lead meetings and people into God encounters and His presence. This is why some cannot do this as they do not have this grace.
- This is required by effective worship leaders.
- People in this grace speak one liners like Author Burt – '*I can do more with the less because of the Greater*" that stops all conversation.

- **Spirit (Breath) of might** --- beyond our strength –
  - Might = force, bravery, mighty acts and deeds

- Place the working and manifestation of the Spirit is released
- Place of God leading us by His Spirit
- Place we move forward in confident faith
- This is the place of activation that creates results.
- This, again, is needed by apostles
- John G. Lake, Smith Wigglesworth and other healing ministries

- **<u>Spirit (Breath) of knowledge</u>** --- not intellect
    - Knowledge = cunning to know the intentions
    - To know the time and season
    - Place of holding fast to promises until manifested.
    - Discerning what is clean and not clean
    - Rightly dividing the Word of God
    - Cannot have the spirit of knowledge without the fear of the Lord because without godly fear, "knowledge puffs up".

- Without the fear of the Lord, knowledge will kill the life of God.
- The spirit of knowledge when applied to all the others creates a multiplying affect.
- Prophets need this grace as well

- **Spirit (Breath) of Holy Fear** --- terror or dread --- awesome reverence,
  - humility,
  - all obedience,
  - willingness to take the lowest place
  - The fear of the Lord is "His delight" **Isaiah 3:3**
    - This is the place that leads to wisdom.
    - This is the place that brings great joy to God because He knows it will lead us to repentance.
  - We saw Charles Finney preach under this grace. Old Time revivalists, some modern evangelists.
  - This is a grace that keeps a move of God on track.

These are not the gifts of the Spirit but these are graces.

- These are Holy Breaths of God released to create change.
- Without the fear of the Lord and the Spirit of the Lord upon us, we cannot come close to God.
    - These are book ends to the graces that lie between.
    - These must first be in place.
    - This is why most of the Body does not move in Throne room grace, they lack the fear of the Lord so the others are not open to them.

Jesus wore these graces as a single woven garment --- like the coat of many colors.

- These graces allow us to have all our limitations removed.
- These graces allow us to break out of anything holding us back!
- These are the embodiment of holiness that can be seen.

His Nature Formed - His Breath Released

Chapter 12

Holiness

Hebrews 12:14 —<u>14 Follow peace with all men, and holiness, without which no man shall see the Lord:</u>

Today we hear so many topics preached over and over but one topic is seldom heard- holiness. We are just not as holy as we think we are. The Bible says to follow holiness which without no man will see God. The current generation desires to see God. The word 'see' means *'with the actual eye'*. It is the word from which we get optometrist. 'Follow' means *'to pursue, run after, to press into'*.

For the most part, we view holiness by definition. 'Holy' means *'to be set part, consecrated'*, etc. It is a process we enter into at salvation. But 'holiness' means *'the process has come to a point of existence or is completed'*. The main reason we seem to be stuck in consecration or sanctification is because we remain at the Cross instead of desiring to go to the Throne. The Cross is more than salvation and freedom from sin. If that was the totality of what it represents, then we are hopeless indeed. The Cross is the beginning of living a holy life to become holiness before God. The Cross focuses on us and the Throne on Him. Many of us would continue in sin or in what we know to be unclean or profane, knowing there is a provision of forgiveness, mercy and grace. The Cross starts a process of becoming clean before God. Whereas the Throne is a present tense 'cleansed'.

So the question is why are we not moving from Cross to Throne, from a process of being holy to a process of holiness? There is a very simple reason. When we see holy and holiness in scripture, we also see these words along side, unclean and profane. We immediately jump to the simple conclusion that we know what is unclean or profane and thus we know what holiness is. It is the opposite of these. But the definition of these words carries far more weight. You see what has happened is we have taken holy things and polluted them. We have made holy things common and thus made them unholy. We do not have reverence for God, His spirit, His word, His worship, His chosen leaders, etc. We have grown accustomed to things and we no longer hold them as valuable. The word 'unclean' also

The Breath of God

means *'to take away honor where honor was once given'*. It means *'to take away the purity of something and make it **COMMMON**'!*

Even the Cross has become common place. Salvation has become simple and all-inclusive instead of exclusive. We have two main types of meetings as Believers, a Cross focus and Spirit focus. A Cross focus on the Son, self, and overcoming problems and sin. The Spirit focus is towards the gifts, manifestations and teaching. We seldom have "Father God" type meetings. (The Father's love meetings such as in Toronto are Cross meetings.) I am talking about the holiness of God, awe-struck, sovereign presence, breath of God type meetings. We love to hang in Cross and Spirit meetings because nothing is really required out of us. We don't have to live a disciplined life to participate. But Father meetings requires only the holy approach. We have seen revivals and moves of God around the Cross and Spirit but not fully around the Father. The awakening that is coming will encompass all three and bring the fullness of Holiness.

The most defining thing of why we no longer see holiness, is things that should be holy are treated as common. We believe meetings and gatherings will just be "common" so we don't attend. We believe there is no value in attending or if we do go, we don't really participate whole heartedly. Our conversations are unholy in gatherings as we talk, not about Kingdom, but what is common. Our actions and our thoughts drift into worldly things. Even that which should be holy, we treat as common such as communion, preaching, and worship. When we look upon the world, we have no standard of holiness, so we view the world differently and define what is unclean not by Biblical terminology but by culturally acceptable terminology. As Leonard Ravenhill put it, "it is no longer adultery, it is having an affair. It is no longer fornication; it is sex outside of marriage. We have taken the sting out of sin". Sin has become too familiar with us. We no longer call things in the world unholy or unclean. We open the door to all to come and join in with a meeting that is supposed to be Holy and we wonder why God is not showing up.

We need to search our hearts and see the places we have made God common. Where have we not shown honor and thus allowed unholiness or that which is unclean to come in? Leaders, preach a message on holiness and see what God will do as you restore things back to being uncommon and clean again!

Hebrews 12:14 (KJV 1900) *Follow peace with all men, and holiness, without which no man shall see the Lord:*

We all desire to see a move of God. What we actually are saying is we want "to see God" Himself. The emerging generation has within their heart a relentless pursuit to experience the things the older generation has already experienced. But for some reason, no matter the amount of fasting and prayer going up, we still are not having breakthrough. Possibly we have put more focus on bearing the name which was an Old Testament focus, than about bearing the nature of God which is a New Testament focus.

Now let me be clear, I am not demeaning the current way many are living their lives. And for many that are in process, there is nothing wrong with them being on the journey. What I am saying is we have many false finish lines of thinking we have attained or no longer need to go deeper in God. We end up living a substandard life without seeing God move or His hand moving. We are touching lives but the ability to change the culture of a nation is sadly lacking. After all, if the Christianity we so cherish and the God we serve so big, then there has to be a degree of the totality of our belief system that can shift a nation in a day!

A generation is crying out for many things in this hour such as hope, fathers, encounters with God, reality of something more than what culture is offering. At the time of this writing, there are more people dying from suicide than car wrecks in America. That to me is astounding that we as a light in darkness are not much more than a flickering light. That is a reflection on the whole of the Body of Christ.

In all honesty, we need a fresh spiritual community to rise up across our nation. We need a community that is founded in holiness and from that advantage point, will be able to confront all things immoral in culture. The soft gospel is not getting the job done and though we may have numbers, we don't have changed hearts so sold out for Christ they are affecting those around them. Numbers are only an indicator of interest and as numbers swell in environments of seeking, it is only an indicator their needs are not being met. God never called us to gather, but to disperse!

The Breath of God

I love how Charles Finney led his meetings. He would preach on the vileness of man and his hardness toward God. He would address the people personally as if he knew them and called them almost every name you could think of: hypocrite, evil, poisoned, etc. At the end of the meeting, he would tell them "You will have no chance for repentance because your heart is not right before God to receive it. But you will come back tomorrow to hear what I have to say." The people would leave grumbling about how he treated them. He looked at it as treating them as sinners. He would do this for several nights, each ending with the denial for repentance. On the fourth or fifth night, when he entered the room, people were crying out for repentance and he then would grant it. The salvations and conversions were deep and lasting and the lives touched in those meetings were impacting to others.

Were the people being drawn because of the abusive words describing them? No, the Holy Spirit was drawing them. But to what, the preaching? No, the nature of God resident in Finney. The people were captivated not by preaching but by the presence he carried. It is said that Finney could board a train and by simply sitting there before the trip was over, everyone on the train would be under conviction.

2 Peter 1:3–4 (KJV 1900) — *3 According as his divine power hath given unto us all things that pertain unto life and godliness, through the knowledge of him that <u>hath called us to glory and virtue</u>: 4 Whereby are given unto us exceeding great and precious promises: that by these ye might <u>be partakers of the divine nature</u>, having escaped the corruption that is in the world through lust.*

We need to be carriers of His nature to this degree today. We need to forsake the program driven, seeker friendly, institutionalized process and realize God's presence will draw them and not our administrative skills. Yes, we will lose some people but if so, then they really were not followers of Christ. Yes, the message of holiness will confront, it has no option but to do so. But God is concerned about what is solid and will remain. The problem is we have repentance with no goal of holiness in mind as a reason for the repentance and much less for the conversions.

In the Old Testament, we were to take on the

name of God. In the New, we are to take on the nature of God. In the Old, there was a consecration process that was followed. In the New Testament, there is a sanctification process. The missing ingredient today is we are only doing consecration and very little sanctification. Consecration is what we decide to do or manage concerning our lives. It is decisions we make and the way we live. It is the first part of a Nazarite vow "to abstain from that which is evil". Sanctification is the process God is allowed to do in our lives. Unlike consecration being mainly outward, sanctification is mainly inward. It is the deep searching of God, deep dealings of God and the correction or chastisement of God. Chastening means *'to teach and correct, to mold the character of a person'*. The correction they received from the natural fathers or leaders produced consecration. This chastisement from the Lord produced sanctification. Read the whole chapter of **Hebrews 12**. The word 'holiness' actually means among other things "*sanctification because of consecration.*" In other words, holiness is the outcome of two things - consecration and sanctification.

1 Thessalonians 3:13 (KJV 1900) — *13 To the*

end he may stablish your hearts unblameable in holiness before God, even our Father, at the coming of our Lord Jesus Christ with all his saints.

So this work is God establishing our hearts or spirits in holiness which is the sanctification process. It is the indwelling Christ imparting holiness to a person. Consecration is our effort as we establish our minds and souls in holiness ---- consecration. Consecration is the yielding to the working of the Holy Spirit. The degree of holiness we will experience is entirely based on the efforts we put forth. He stamps us as sanctified BECAUSE OF consecration. If you are waiting for God to just come and make you holy, you will have a long wait. He tells us repeatedly in scripture to consecrate so He can sanctify.

Today we have many next generation structures who are only dealing with consecration or living a consecrated life. But we are still at the first part of a Nazarite vow. The second part is the key, "to also abstain from that which is good as well as things that might distract." In the effort to gain followers, we have said it is alright to do those things. Hence we are seeing the effects of God's Spirit (consecration) but not God Himself (sanctification or holiness). Even Jesus told the parable of a man who bought land, another got married, and another man purchased oxen. All good things, noble things, and needed things, but all asked to be excused. Jesus did not run after them to convince them but turned and sought a new group of those who would not just be consecrated but sanctified, the marriage of the Lamb, a holy encounter of intimacy.

Holiness is what caused Jesus to be resurrected. The holiness upon Jesus kept Him from being corrupted by death. It is what allowed Jesus access into the Throne room to both see and hear the Father. It is what makes commitment (which is lacking in the *Ecclesia*) dedication, a loss of reputation, boldness, confidence, and vessels carrying both messages from heaven and virtue from the nature of God.

Exodus 28:36 (KJV 1900) *And thou shalt make a plate of pure gold, and grave upon it, like the engravings of a signet, HOLINESS TO THE LORD.*

We are to be called holiness to the Lord. Consecration is for us but holiness is for Him! We are not seeing the move of God because we are only consecrated and not truly sanctified. But God is working with vessels willing to go on the journey. Many are being dealt with in this hour of true holiness. This state of being must first come before the message of holiness will flow out. Perhaps if we could see briefly what this will produce, we might be more willing. Holiness, not consecration, will heal the breach of generations, heal the earth's cry, heal the breach between cultures and social injustice, heal the breach in the *Ecclesia* and heal the breach in men's hearts.

Spiritual vs. Holy

What is stopping this holiness is a misconception we have concerning what is truly the focus of God's heart. We have misinterpreted this to strive to be spiritual. We do all kinds of spiritual acrobatics and flexing of spiritual exercises. But there is a big difference between being spiritual and being holy. Spirituality can refer to an ultimate or an alleged immaterial reality. It is a source of inspiration or orientation or even the search for the absolute of God. There are many things that are spiritual, occultism, rituals, witchcraft, etc. Spirituality can even be participating in an anointing that comes upon you. But holiness is participating with the Spirit living inside you. Spirituality is an outward expression while holiness is an inward working. You can give me a spiritual reason for your actions, saying all the right words of why you made certain decisions or missed a meeting because of a so called assignment which really was nothing more than your own flesh deciding something and then justifying it by being spiritual. But can we give answers that are holy? Can people give a holy answer of why they are leaving a ministry or justifying their actions or lack of commitment or unwillingness to do what is being asked of them? A holy answer will allow all to participate. A spiritual answer only allows a few. Spiritual actions have little to no conviction, thus little to no change. Spiritual actions will wear us out and cause us to become disheartened because of the lack of results produced. But true holiness will convict people to the core. It may not be popular but will have measurable results and change. We have become so dull to the Holy Spirit's conviction because of our spiritual acts. We believe we are equal to instead of realizing we actually have hardened our heart. If you can weep for souls then your heart is still soft towards God's conviction. If you respond, not caring what others think, then you are on the path to sanctification and holiness.

Seducing Spirits

The spiritual battle is on to keep us in the constant place of consecration and not sanctification. The enemy knows if we stay busy making decisions and working in our own strength, then he has control of us, the Church, and thus holds the world. If we will move past the place of consecration and truly be sanctified, then we will no longer fight so many things as they will be settled issues and the Spirit of Holiness would flow from us. The battle is about souls, destiny, identity, etc. but actually the battle is against God's Holiness. The separation that holiness brings in a person's life settles the issue that demonic forces cannot touch that person any longer. There are three tests we must all pass in this hour that are connected with seducing spirits. The same three tests Jesus had to pass in **Luke 4** and that Paul spelled out for us in **1 John**

2:16. They are the lust of the eyes, the lust of the flesh, and the pride of life. I feel we have done or are doing fairly well with the first two which are consecration but the pride of life is truly sanctification. Spiritual pride is a huge issue in this hour. Many think they know all they need to learn and are no longer in need of a teacher, yet their lives are producing little to no fruit. Many think there is no need for others. They do spiritual acts but not acts of holiness which convicts to the point of change. Many are content with how they are living. Many are making decisions to place other things before God and that spiritual pride is keeping us from truly seeing God! It is saying 'I am not in need of anything' and is a rejection of God and His holiness. It is now becoming more easy for me to see the "spiritual" person as I am looking for the holiness of God. Before I understood this, I was looking for the "spiritual" not realizing just how shallow it really is.

We are either being led by God's Spirit or allowing seducing spirits to have a role in our lives. Leaders, many of our people are being influenced by seducing spirits. They are working through the lust of the eyes, the lust of the flesh, and the pride of life. It is truly what Paul said in **1 Tim 4:1**.

1 Timothy 4:1-3 (KJV 1900) *Now the Spirit speaketh expressly, that in the latter times some shall depart from the faith, giving heed to seducing spirits, and doctrines of devils; Speaking lies in hypocrisy; having their conscience seared with a hot iron; Forbidding to marry, and commanding to abstain from meats, which God hath created to be received with thanksgiving of them which believe and know the truth.*

This verse in Greek reads something like this*: in the fulfillment or conclusion of the Kairos or a divine moment of God, some shall withdraw themselves, keep away from, stand off from, the place where the conviction of truth is being expressed, and will bring near to their minds, be addicted to, and attend their selfishness, by misleading, wandering, leading into error spirits, who instruct as messengers of satan with condemnation giving them statements they make as their own as they become imposters impersonating others.*

This is the ultimate goal of all demonic spirits;

it is their plan that connects all activity together they all are working towards as a unified force. It is not saying there is a singular spirit of seduction but that all demonic spirits seduce. I find it amazing the first level of this seduction is the withdrawing of the person from the place that truth and conviction of truth exists. How strategic! As a leader, I have seen this occur repeatedly and it is still occurring as people's commitment to be in a gathering is lacking. I can only conclude one thing, that a spirit is convincing them of something. The second occurrence is to get them focused on themselves. The word to 'Heed' actually is associated with selfish desires, self centeredness, which equates to spiritual pride. There is a convincing in the mind that justifies. After all, the source of conviction has been removed. The third attack then comes as false doctrine is infused. The outcome is actually a hypocritical display, the mimicking of others' statements and words and they become false.

For us, as leaders, to be aware of how this demonic activity occurs is one thing. The second is how we stop it. I have one answer and only one answer, that as leaders, we <u>must</u>

have a greater degree of holiness upon us. Only consecrating people or leading them into consecration will not hold them. It must be a heart searching from God. Holiness will have deep conviction but release deep waves of grace as well. Good messages will cause people to desire things but also become frustrated when things do not move or materialize. Holiness will always create things deeply in people and then virtue will flow out of them. The life of God will be seen, felt and experienced. Remember holiness will not allow corruption to touch it. We must challenge our people to move from consecration to true holiness so they may be kept from the evil one.

Holiness is drawn to the nature of God because holiness _is_ the nature of God. And the nature of God is drawn to holiness because God is the nature of holiness. Now that's a lot to mediate on! But the stark reality is you cannot separate the nature of God from holiness or have holiness apart from His nature. Thus if we look around and say we desire to have His nature, we must truly desire His holiness as well. Holiness is going to confront us to the very core of our being. It will cause a great internal wrestling. It will also cause a great reward of the splendor of His nature being formed in us.

When we begin to reflect on the holiness that is evident in heaven, especially when reading the twelfth chapter of Hebrews, it is quite a thing. We sing, pray and ask for God to descend from such a holy place and visit us, but we also ask Him to take up residence and dwell among us! Yet He chooses to do so, not so much starting out in a corporate gathering, but in the heart of individuals. As these individuals who have set themselves apart gather in larger groups, then His presence and nature comes to truly dwell in a corporate body. Holiness is a radiant purity that is a reflection of God.

In essence, He dwells within us. When we ask God to descend, we are in actuality saying "we have made this place look and feel like heaven so You would feel welcome to be here as well!" Our meetings and hearts have to go a ways for that to really be a reality but yet in times past, as people reached into these areas of complete sanctification, God did come and dwell.

Holiness supersedes all things because holiness is the place from which all things were created. If it is His nature, then from His nature or holiness creative miracles flow. You see, there is a certain degree of holiness needed for miracles and anything creative to come into existence. It is because we are drawing from holiness or His nature to bring something into being that did not exist. It is the act of calling things that are not as though they are.

Hebrews 2:4 tells us the Trinity produces an outcome from the place of holiness. **The Son** produces the nature that is the carrier of holiness. **The Holy Spirit** produces manifestations from holiness: signs, wonders, miracles and gifts to equip to overcome, from the place of holiness. **The Father produces** the breath of life that sovereignty creates and sustains all things from the temporal to the eternal state through holiness. You see all things do exist by Him, through Him and for Him. Another way of saying it is anything that is eternal will come from holiness, by holiness and exist for holiness purposes.

But the greatest thing holiness will do is it will cause in us a moral dilemma. This means it will create decision points in our life of evaluations and change. It will cause us to truly measure ourselves and compare ourselves by His standards of righteousness and for the most part, expose our lack or misconceptions. But it will also show forth the places of victory and success we have had in overcoming and walking in victory. For most people who have allowed God's dealings through life, they end up with one final thing that must give way to have complete and total surrender and to be more than a conqueror, to be an over comer. Holiness will have patience for this final battle but will also pursue until a willing heart is formed.

Holiness will produce in us a cultural dilemma as well for what we will deem as acceptable or not. At the time of this writing, I find myself communicating with several leaders who cannot believe the condition of so many worship leaders who are drinking and having no real sanctification process at work in their lives. I have been in contact with some worship leaders as well who are deeply broken over what has been allowed/ tolerated for the sake of "the show" and the demands of the people. We have compromised so drastically to please people that we no longer know what pleases God. Holiness will produce in us an unwillingness to be a participant in what is unclean. We will deny it room and confront it head on no matter the consequences. Holiness will cause our heart to ache and be burdened with what we see, instead of accepting it and even participating in it.

Holiness grips our hearts to the same degree sin gripped our heart before salvation. That is why Paul said he was apprehended by Christ. He was gripped with the new nature he had received and how the old nature no longer existed. God did not just redeem us or set us free from sin to go to heaven or to be in liberty. He actually calls us to holiness so His nature is dominant in our lives.

We saw Isaiah had a divine invitation to enter in **Isaiah 6:1**, the angelic host said "Holy Holy Holy". There was a pronouncement of holiness decreed over Isaiah. He could not enter in to the encounter until the decree was spoken. The decreeing of holiness enlarged the opening of heaven so he could enter in. It made the entrance point much more accessible. Imagine today if we have entrance points established in our nation of this kind of holiness and decreeing of holiness! Imagine the impact this would make on the Body of Christ!

Isaiah saw himself as unclean. The holiness confronted him deep inside. It was not about his lips but about his heart. Out of the abundance of the heart, the mouth speaks. His confession was a confession of heart. But God's answer was to touch him with a coal from the altar. Now to see the depth of the holiness of heaven. This altar in heaven, accessible to angels, was so holy that the holy angel took a tong to take the coal. The angel could not touch the coal in the chance of touching the altar. This is the same altar mentioned in Hebrews that says the blood of Christ touched. But that holy coal touched Isaiah, it was able to touch humanity! I hope you see the high privilege we have in holiness.

Holiness defined Christ. It allowed both the nature of God to be formed and the power of God to be displayed. It allowed the Resurrection to occur, because Jesus was holy, He could not see corruption. It was holiness that sustained Him in death. Holiness has a power that is greater than all other spiritual dynamics!

2 Corinthians 7:1 (KJV 1900) — *1 Having therefore these promises, dearly beloved, let us cleanse ourselves from all filthiness of the flesh and spirit, <u>perfecting holiness in the fear of God</u>.*

So when is holiness seen as perfected? Holiness is perfected when we finally have Godly fear. A healthy reverence, respect and honor. When we truly begin to take charge and are willing to be held responsible for our actions. When we commit to being consecrated and then sanctified. It is bringing forth what is expected from your life and living your life for God over your ambitions. It is **<u>passing the same three tests Christ passed in Luke 4.</u>** The lust of the flesh, the lust of the eyes and the Pride of Life also found in **1 John 2:16**.

You see holiness (sanctification) --- in (the fixed position we maintain) the fear of God will keep you from sin, transgression, and iniquity. It will cause you be to be effective in:

1. Healing the breach of generations --- fathering and Sonship
    a. We see this with David and Solomon

b. Moses and Joshua
   c. Paul and Timothy

2. Healing the breach in the earth --- **Romans 8**
   a. The earth's cry for sons to manifest
   b. The Church's cry for the fathers to manifest

3. Healing the breach between cultures- Acts, Cross Cultural ministry teams
   a. Racism
   b. Poverty and the poor

4. Healing the breach in the *Ecclessia* -- Jesus' prayer to be "one"
   a. Doctrinal divisions
   b. Theological interpretations
   c. Institutional function

5. Healing the breach in men's hearts
   a. Broken heartedness
   b. Deliverance
   c. Signs and wonders
   d. A new Birth of Freedom

His Nature Formed - His Breath Released

Chapter 13

The Journey Begins

So the burning questions you hopefully have are "How do we get the breath of God into our lives?" "How does the nature of God expand ever increasingly?" These are probably two very hard questions to be resolved. As with all things in God, there is not one real answer but we must go back to principles and see the things we must be pursuing.

We all have the beginning stages of the first found in **Isaiah 11:1-3 *the Spirit of the Lord is upon us***. This occurs at the time that we are born again. Our spirit is rejuvenated in the Lord and a restoration process begins in our life. He does make all things new and old things have passed away, but our mind and patterns and habits of life are constantly trying to tell us to the contrary. We are under a battle in our mind to be convinced of the reality that our spirit already knows. For many people as the Spirit of the Lord is now upon them, they seem to settle in this one area and not move much beyond the point of salvation or the liberty of being free from sin. It is the same Spirit that raised Christ from the dead that is dwelling within us. The same resurrection power is resident. God is no respecter of persons and what He has given to one; He will give to all that receive Him.

2 Peter 1:4 (KJV 1900) — 4 *Whereby are given unto us exceeding great and precious promises: that by these <u>ye might be partakers of the divine nature,</u> having escaped the corruption that is in the world through lust*.

But, just how we experience salvation is also one way the remaining natures of Christ would come upon us. When we were yet sinners, we saw the need for Christ in our life. We saw the areas of our life that were lacking and had to come to a decision point to accept the provision that He made for us. Our response was to repent and change the course of our life concerning the things that we knew were detrimental and not pleasing to God. We simply by faith accepted what He had done for us and received it as our own. Each time will require seeing our lack, coming to a decision point, and repenting for the way we have conducted our life in many areas.

The Breath of God

Just as salvation is an ongoing process of deliverance and change and not a onetime event, so is receiving the natures of God and having His breath come upon us. It must become a lifestyle of us staying in a constant pursuit of His presence in our lives and allowing His presence to be ever-expanding. The only way I can describe it is to be living in an awareness of God and His intentions.

For myself, I may not feel the most spiritual at times, or the most studied out and prepared, or even the most prayed up. But one thing I have trained myself in is to be sensitive to the Holy Spirit. Sensitivity to the Holy Spirit comes over time and cherishing His activity and actions in our life. You can have the most messed up day, feel totally unspiritual and the sensitivity to the Holy Spirit will enable you to suddenly just step into the spiritual realm. The spiritual realm is always stable no matter how we feel or the circumstances of life that are occurring around us. If we look at the life of Jesus and Paul and many others in the spiritual dynamics that they moved in, if they were based upon everything going perfect around them, we never would have had anything occur to be written down in the Bible.

For the breath of God to flow through you and out of you and come from that nature deep inside, the main requirement is really your yieldedness to the Holy Spirit. The deeper the yielding, the greater the potential for the breath to be released and the drawing from the deep, within you, to be done. The second thing that I've always done is be willing to let the Holy Spirit use me no matter what. Be it a prophetic word, praying for somebody, or finding answers for someone's problems in counseling, I've always been willing to yield and that willingness in the simple things or the moving of the gifts of the Spirit has enabled the deeper things to be released out of my life.

Exodus 33:11 (KJV 1900) — *11 And the LORD spake unto Moses face to face, as a man speaketh unto his friend. And he turned again into the camp: but his servant Joshua, the son of Nun, a young man, departed not out of the tabernacle.*

Deuteronomy 34:10 (KJV 1900) — *10 And there arose not a prophet since in Israel like unto Moses, whom the LORD knew face to face,*

The Breath of God

You see, one of the things that seem to occur is a relationship with God has deepened to a new level. And we see Moses ascend the mountain of the Lord to fellowship with God. The Bible says that Moses talked to God face-to-face. Yet the Bible also says that no man has seen God and lived. How did Moses talk to God face-to-face then? Did he actually see the face of God, or is he so close to God that he was receiving His breath through the cloud of His glory? I believe God's breath was so close that not only did he receive it into his spirit, but it blew across him even to the point that his countenance changed.

Genesis 32:30 (KJV 1900) — *30 And Jacob called the name of the place Peniel: for I have seen God face to face, and my life is preserved.*

Ezekiel 20:35 (KJV 1900) — *35 And I will bring you into the wilderness of the people, and there will I plead with you face to face.*

Judges 6:22 (KJV 1900) — *22 And when Gideon perceived that he was an angel of the LORD, Gideon said, Alas, O Lord GOD! for because I have seen an angel of the LORD face to face.*

His Nature Formed - His Breath Released

These face-to-face meetings with God were more than just the time of conversation and exchange of words. I believe they were times that God came and breathed upon those leaders to receive His nature and the grace that goes with that nature for the assignment that was before them.

You see, each one of us has a set assignment given by God while here upon the earth. We have been given certain giftings and abilities- both spiritual and natural. These all are designed as tools in our arsenal to not only provide and make our way in life but also to advance the Kingdom of God. These advances are contingent upon us understanding our tools and how it implement them. We can do much in our own strength and abilities but when we encounter the nature of God, our abilities and supernatural gifting are infused with His creative power and force that only comes from His nature. That is why Moses could part the Red Sea, Samson could destroy the temple, and others could do great exploits. It was both that anointing and a favor of God <u>upon</u> them and the nature and breath of God coming <u>from </u>them.

What I know is this, that the greater degree of

the nature and breath of God required, the greater degrees of us emptying ourselves from pride and all things that stand between us and God. We actually can reach a state that the things of this world will grow faintly dim and have no hold on us.

It requires sanctification and the internal conflict of wrestling with things in our lives we might not want to give up. As I write this, I am in contact with many leaders in this place of wrestling. Wrestling not with sin issues so much as wrestling with time and affection issues. Things that are fine but rob time with God. Each person's journey is different and will require different decisions to be made. What is really happening is new values are emerging and along with that, a whole new set of possibilities.

These require a dividing away from our lives, thus it is called a sanctification process. It is a process. The nature of God is not formed in us in a moment or a prayer line. It is formed as we give way to more and more of the Spirit of God's desires. It is what we seldom hear preached anymore and it's called Lordship. But I call it 'yielded Lordship. The difference being one can be lip service and the other requires heart action.

Lordship is a large topic. It covers all areas of our walk and life. It touches how we make decisions and how we decide to walk out the truth we have been given. It is what separates a new believer to become a disciple. It is what finishes a disciple to be Christ-like. After all, Christ was under the Lordship of His Father. Lordship is about submission to God and His desires for us. Without it, we have no real spiritual authority. With it, we have all of heaven backing our every move.

Lordship is all about the nature of Christ being formed in us. It is about willingness in our heart because we love God more than ourselves and we are willing to submit ourselves to Him. It is understanding truth that He has our best interest in store in all areas of our life and He understands that, beginning to the end. It is trusting Him with more than meeting our needs; it is trusting Him with completing the work in our lives. It is about transferring the ownership of our heart and exchanging it so that He owns our heart.

Of all the things that Jesus talked about,

The Breath of God

Lordship was an underlying theme hidden in almost every conversation. He was not so much concerned about salvation but knew that if Lordship was not in place; salvation would become an empty act. He was more concerned about finishing strong in life and preparing us for ruling and reigning in all of eternity. Without the Lordship issue settled while we are here on the earth, our chances of being assigned a ruler ship in heaven become slimmer and slimmer. God is not only looking at how the Lordship will be acted out while we're here upon the earth, but also the effects of it that we would carry into all of eternity.

As we all examine and evaluate our results of our spiritual life, we easily see and realize the areas that are lacking. Even though we can cover this up around others and even hold some things in secret, we still know ourselves way better than we care to. This evaluation is also the sanctification process. A hard, healthy look at our lives and then dealing with what the Holy Spirit is pointing out for us to change is part of the process of the nature of God being formed. Some of the things we're willing to deal with and it is easy for us to embrace those dealings and the changes that come with it. The other things that we might be unwilling to deal with, we will put off. These things God will still come back around to, at a later date and re-address in our lives.

This nature will require a shifting in our value systems and where our time and energy is placed. I can't tell you how many leaders I am talking to that this is a place of shifting what they are doing. They can no longer fill time with things that are of no eternal value. What is happening is a generation of leaders is rising who have been around for several years, not compromising, holding fast and in pursuit of the deeper things of God. They are seeing their lives and saying, *"God, there has to be more! There has to be something of greater value than all the things I have been doing"*.

I know of one prominent, nationally known, and well recognized leader who slowly slipped away from speaking at conferences to writing articles and books. He now spends time with God in such a dynamic way in his home, he has shifted to inviting others to come and sit before God with him. Those who go, say the presence of God in this man's home is almost unbearable as holiness is permeating everything. Some come through the door and begin to weep uncontrollably. Others are awe struck and say nothing. This leader has invited them into a way of living that he has established and is modeling. He feels his role is to be faithful and bring other leaders into this intense encounter with the presence of God. He feels that the nature of God coming more and more resident within the leaders is the key to bringing the presence of God more fully into the Body of Christ.

One of the things that is required to fully have the nature of God established in our lives is a constant pursuing of Him. We must move from the casual encounters of where we've all been to God and His presence, to the place that we are dissatisfied unless His presence is saturating the environment we're in.

Exodus 33:13–18 (KJV 1900) 13 Now therefore, I pray thee, if I have found grace in thy sight, shew me now thy way, that I may know thee, that I may find grace in thy sight: and consider that this nation is thy people. 14 And he said, My presence shall go with thee, and I will give thee rest. 15 And he said unto him, If thy presence go not with me, carry us not up hence. 16 For wherein shall it be known here that I and thy people have found grace in thy sight? is *it not in that thou goest with us? so shall we be separated, I and thy people, from all the people that are upon the face of the earth. 17 And the LORD said unto Moses, I will do this thing also that thou hast spoken: for thou hast <u>found grace in my sight, and</u> I know thee by name. 18 And he said, I beseech thee, <u>shew me thy glory.</u>*

The first thing that Moses asked was that he would be showed the ways of God but also that he could find grace in God's sight. Moses knew the only way to fully take advantage of God's grace and favor resting upon him was to understand <u>the reason why</u> grace was there. The Lord's response was remarkable and He said that His presence would go with him. What more could a person ask for than the presence of God to always be with us? As the presence of God is near us, so is the nature of God surrounding us. Then Moses' response was quite a remarkable response, he basically said, God it's all about Your presence and if your presence is not leading us that we can go. The second question that Moses asked God was if he could see His Glory. He was testing to see just how far this grace is upon our life. There is a grace for us to go deeper with God. God actually desires for us to go on a journey in this grace to understand Him. God answered the next day and took him to the mount and showed him ALL GLORY as it passed before him.

David pursued God, Paul pursued God, and almost all the men we read about in historic Christianity had come to a point of ultimately God instead of pursuing knowledge or the gifts of the Spirit, or followers. They began a relentless pursuit of God and ended with Gods nature. Paul said in **Phil. 3:10** "*that I may know him*". Paul was after something more than the casual relationship, he wanted an intimate one. Once you realize the nature of God is resident within you, you understand, then that you do indeed know Him. Your perspective changes about the environment around you and an unwillingness to embrace sin and the foolishness of the world becomes your portion.

We are in an age of religious complexity - the simplicity of Christ and the pursuit of Him is not seen much. We pursue worship music, programs, accolades of 'me', words of affirmation, and selfish desire. This all brings us to the conclusion of shallow logic, low standards, works mentality, and a self-serving gospel to meet our every need. Gone is the suffering and great anguish of soul as we wrestle with ourselves and the worldliness around us. All the while God wants us to possess nothing but Him. That which you constantly pursue to possess, will constantly own you once you possess it.

The closeness to God that we desire is a deep desire placed in the very core of all men, put in place by God Himself. It is a desire that runs so deep our human abilities and pursuit of happiness will never touch it. It is a desire to return to the first state of glory that we knew; the state before the foundations of the earth. It is a desire to return to the creative power of God that was as the first. It is a desire to have an unbroken relationship with God. After all, that in essence is what the fullness of the nature of God is. We are living our lives to such a degree that we are never out of relationship with Him or feeling isolated from Him.

This pursuit has no limitations or boundaries. We can stop at any time and decide we have had enough or we can continue even deeper. But the beckoning of God is always present for us to come and tarry a while, or to answer the call where deep calls to deep or extreme calls to extreme.

For me, the greatest times of pursuit yielded the deepest revelations and the deepest work of God in my life. I have been on several short fasts of 7-14 days, numerous 21 day fasts and a few 40 day fasts. I must say of all those experiences, the 40 day fasts were the most exhilarating as you can feel God's presence so close and at times sense Him carrying you. My spiritual senses were so in tune and I was hearing God's voice so precisely. I could tell you who was going to show at meetings, I knew when the phone would ring and who it would be minutes before and even the topic of discussion.

But in all of the times of fasting and pursuing, intimacy was truly found, it deepened and remained. It was times of great revelation as God shared His heart with me. It was also times of His nature inside me growing and expanding. Fasting is a privilege and there has to be a certain grace. When I fast, I ask God for the privilege of fasting and permission to do so. I then know there is a purpose I have engaged into while fasting and an outcome. Fasting is never to move God's hand but it is always to change us. It repositions us and resets us spiritually. You see privileges only come through intimacy because attached to privilege, is an entrustment of stewardship.

Pursuing God and attaining the nature of Christ is the ability to know we are living in ascended life awareness. The nature of God puts us into great advantage in everyday life and the words coming from us are more confident and sure. They are filled with faith and power. We begin to see that when Christ arose, we arose as well and not in a future tense of our death, but in the present tense of how we live our lives. It is living in the glorified state that we once knew at the time of Adam. It is a great exchange we have made, the nature of Christ for ours.

We must pursue God's presence before we pursue God's purposes. What we generally pursue is fame and recognition, and the moving of the Holy Spirit. But without His presence in our own lives, we could even stand to lose our life. Jesus said it did not matter about the things we did, but whether we really knew Him. In **John 17:2-3**, Jesus spoke of eternal life and said to know "***the only true God, and Jesus Christ, whom thou hast***

sent." It is not a prayer said in an altar call, it is not a change of lifestyle or way of living. It is not even repentance from sin and living a good moral life. It is a state of being found in HIM. Not just occupying some space but actually truly knowing Him!

The journey should and must lead us to the ultimate positioning of our lives and that being a deep uniting with Christ. We should end at the place of oneness that Jesus talked about in **John 17**. This oneness is not unity as so many have thought it to be. Unity is part of it but not the definition to be settled on. Unity implies mutual agreement that has occurred and it can occur because of compromise or exchanging ideas or concepts until there is agreement. But the oneness talked about in John that Jesus is looking for is the Greek word *Heis* which means '*first, unique, only, uniqueness, organic in thought process* – not solitary but bound and united to the many because of what binds them, they are bound to'. It is a binding of natures, Christ to ours and ours to Christ until we are bound in Name - **John 17:11**, Word- **John 17:20**, Glory – **John 17:22** and Perfection- **John 17:23**. This oneness really comes down to- that we might be bound together by common cause or by being united with Christ. What better way to fully be united with Him and each other than to have His nature!

(For an in-depth study of **John 17**, see my book <u>Kingdom Discipleship</u> page 171.)

Finally, it will require holiness. Without holiness, no man will see God. Since holiness is such a large area to cover, we will explore its interaction with the nature of God and how holiness is to play a role in our lives in the next chapter.

Chapter 14

The Challenge

By now you have seen a lot of great insights into the nature of God and His breath. But there is still one more insight that you need. It's probably the hardest one to come to grips with and causes lots of internal conflict. Once it is understood, this entire book will make more sense and you probably will want to reread it.

What insight is that? It's about yourself. Imagine that! I am going to talk about our human nature for a moment. The thing is everything we have been discussing concerning God's nature, sanctification, holiness and ministering from a much deeper place has a common point that must be addressed. That is the dying of our flesh; the crucifying of our desires and even our value system for they are not aligned with God's desires and plans for our lives.

You see, we never change how we function unless we first shift an area of our value system to make room for the change. But the changes of our value systems are generally not an easy thing to accomplish. It touches areas we have put energy and investment into. It makes us look at things we thought were settled. It also shows our lack and potential that was not tapped. Many times we might have to deal with things attached to that value system such as friends, associations, soul ties, and our own pride. Perhaps we are just settled into our Christianity and are waiting for some great move of God to come so we can go deeper then.

The nature of God is something you cannot be taught to delve into. No matter how much I have given you in this book, I could not teach you into it. I can only show you the benefits of it through sharing my journey so you would desire it for yourself. You can study and study, but you have to pause and allow God to deal with you in a deeper dealing than ever before. The studying will lead you into deeper things but it will require decision upon decisions and one of the main ones is determining not to stop or settle for a false finish line.

It is not something you can have hands laid on and receive it. If we could do that then the process is thwarted and it would be so easy that there would be no value. We can receive prayer for the removal of obstacles in our lives and we can agree for greater understanding. But the nature of God and His breath cannot be attained by simply standing in a prayer line. Nor can a person be talked into it or counseled into it. Counseling may help identify and remove hindrances but ultimately a person has to be responsible for their own life. What we are really talking about is to live a disciplined life. A discipline that has accountability to others but also has enough tenacity and spiritual strength to lead a disciplined lifestyle that is not dependent on outside influences to hold us in place. A discipline that also has an ongoing awareness of what could and will be detrimental to the disciplines already in place or forming.

Paul said in **Philippians 3: 12** that he had not already attained the Resurrection or perfection but that he was following after to be apprehended by Christ. The overall context is back to verse **10** to know Him in the power of the Resurrection. We won't know this unless we have died and Paul was not talking about the end of his life on earth but a spiritual encounter of the death of himself. The word 'power' here is the word *dunamis* which means *'the very nature residing inside the person'.*

The fellowship of his suffering. The word 'fellowship' means *'association and communion'*. This could hold several meanings. *Suffering for righteousness*, or *suffering for the Gospels' sake*, or *suffering because of our circumstances*. But maybe it means *suffering with internal conflict that Christ be formed in us*. To be made conformable to His death even gives us more insight of the process. 'Conformable' means *'to have the same exact form'*! This is a focus of being made in the likeness of Christ and having His nature to the degree that we would come to the end of ourselves and allow God's will to fully flow through us.

I know several people who are pressing into the nature of God and His breath. They have forsaken fame and the flattery of men. They seek no position but to be before God's face. They desire nothing of this world and have separated themselves from it in many ways. They have become "in this world but not of it." I, too, am still on the journey and not where I want to be, but at least I'm in the process. You will know when you are in the journey as well because of a deep awareness in your spirit.

The Breath of God

There will be a settledness of the process occurring in you.

So the question is: will you take the challenge? Will you go on the journey with me into a great place in God? I am not saying you must make this giant leap but I am challenging you to take some strong steps. Allow yourself to yield into God's dealings. Be the nature of God on the earth and see the breath of life being released from your life. This is the awakening that is coming and God is looking for those with His nature to carry His breath to release the final move on the earth!

His Nature Formed - His Breath Released

About the author

Greg Crawford has been active in ministry for over 30 years serving in almost every type of leadership role. He is the founder of Jubilee International Ministries which recently relocated to Des Moines, Iowa. He and his wife, Julie, have also co-labored in founding Jubilee School of Ministry and Jubilee International School of Ministry which now has 40+ schools in developing nations. The International School network graduates roughly 5,000 students yearly. They have grown the network of schools to stand on their own within their nation without ongoing support from the United States. Jubilee School of Ministry in the USA has international graduates who have established schools and ministry works in many nations of the world as well. Many have planted churches, orphanages, and are involved in high places of influence in governments. Today Jubilee School of Ministry is no longer a class room but is an online school of ministry training with over 350 hours of online instruction.

Apostle Crawford or APG, as he is known by his spiritual children, has traveled on numerous international trips, leading teams into nations conducting leadership conferences. He has worked in Cote d' Ivoire, Nigeria, South Africa, Zambia, and Indonesia. Many of the nations have had reoccurring trips as he has taken teams of ministers with him. He laid the ground work for the apostolic reformation in Nigeria with close to 12 trips to this nation alone, teaching thousands of leaders on team ministry and the apostolic for the first time. With close to 50 ministers ordained under them in the United States, they also provide counsel and insight, helping many church leaders today.

Apostle Crawford has become a spiritual father to many and has a desire to see the generations running together as one voice. He has labored to see the Kingdom expression of reformation and awakening come by travels in Iowa and the United States to help bring this into existence. He is best known for his revelatory teaching style and has a unique and powerful ministry of laying on of hands for impartation. He carries a deep message that releases the breath of God to confront the hearts of believers. This has opened the door for him to speak at national conferences. The revelatory dynamic has enabled him to write several books, write close to 300 hours of classes, some taught by secular colleges, and to send out a bi-monthly teaching through email. His teachings can be found on many websites and have been the lead feature article on Identity Network a leading prophetic voice in America with a web base following of close to 350,000.

He holds a PHD of Ministry which he

received Magna Suma Cum Laude. He is ordained with Jim Hodges' Federation of Ministers and Churches International and is in relationship with several national voices. Currently he is overseeing The BASE, a ministry located in Des Moines, IA, to bring awakening and reformation to the Church and culture. The forerunner ministry of the BASE has creative spontaneous worship, gifts and callings development, investment by spiritual fathering, and revelatory instruction with opportunity. More information can be found at the ministry website **www.thebaseiowa.org**

His Nature Formed - His Breath Released

Other Resources

Greg Crawford's Blog

Blog --- http://thebaseiowa.wordpress.com/

Books on Amazon or For Kindle Download
on Greg Crawford's Author page.

http://www.amazon.com/-/e/B00BEGN362

   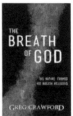

  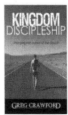 

His Nature Formed - His Breath Released

Made in the USA
Columbia, SC
16 October 2018